Ms. Loretta
2419 Univ
Ruskin, Fl

W9-BQW-015

THE WOMAN'S
NEW SELLING GAME

THE WOMAN'S
NEW SELLING GAME

How to Sell Yourself—and Anything Else

Carole Hyatt

McGraw-Hill

New York   San Francisco   Washington, D.C.   Auckland   Bogotá
Caracas   Lisbon   London   Madrid   Mexico City   Milan
Montreal   New Delhi   San Juan   Singapore
Sydney   Tokyo   Toronto

Library of Congress Cataloging-in-Publication Data

Hyatt, Carole
    The woman's new selling game / by Carole Hyatt
        p.   cm.
    ISBN 0-07-031828-X
    1. Selling. 2. Businesswomen. I. Title.
HF5438.25.H89   1998
658.85'082—dc21   97-25257
                                          CIP

McGraw-Hill

A Division of The McGraw·Hill Companies

Copyright © 1998 by The McGraw-Hill Companies. All rights reserved. Printed in the United States of America. Except as permitted under the United States Copyright Act of 1976, no part of this publication may be reproduced or distributed in any form or by any means, or stored in a data base or retrieval system, without the prior written permission of the publisher.

    3   4   5   6   7   8   9   0   FGR/FGR   9   0   2   1   0   9   8

ISBN 0-07-031828-X

The sponsoring editor for this book was Betsy N. Brown, the editing supervisor was Fred Dahl, and the production supervisor was Pamela Pelton. It was set in Fairfield by Inkwell Publishing Services.

McGraw-Hill books are available at special quantity discounts to use as premiums and sales promotions, or for use in corporate training programs. For more information, please write to the Director of Special Sales, McGraw-Hill, 11 West 19th Street, New York, NY 10011. Or contact your local bookstore.

 This book is printed on recycled, acid-free paper containing a minimum of 50% recycled, de-inked fiber.

CONTENTS

PREFACE

This book belongs to you, and to the scores of women and men we interviewed who so generously shared their thoughts and experiences with you. Their stories are the lifeblood of The Selling Game, the flesh and marrow of the anatomy of success.

Although their names and locales have been changed to spare any possible embarrassment, I wish to express my sincere personal thanks to "Alma," "Beth," "Doris," and all the rest who helped make this book a valuable guide for us all.

I am especially grateful to the original interviewees: Joan Alevras, Elinor Bunin, Denise Cavanaugh, Lois Clark, Pat Cush, Lisa Dubin, Dina Dubois, Dorothea Elman, Belie Frank, Mya Gowdy, Selina Guber, LaQuita Henry, Suzanne Jeffers, Enid Johnson, Judy Katz, Barbara Lee, Marian Maged, Arthur Mayer, Joan Phillips, Judy Price, Shelley Rappaport, Jackie Reinach, Albert Sanders, Carolyn Setlow, Diane Sharron, Tina Spiro, Lit Van Fatten, Margot Wellington, Lynda Wessel, Av Westin, Kathleen Westin, Peter Woronoff, and Elaina Zuker.

To my constant sources of stories, shared experiences, and counsel, thank you's to Arnold Brown, Christa Dowling, Nancy Drosd, Lee Elman, Elly Guggenheimer, Sonya Hamlin, Dennis and Nancy Pelz-Paget, Barbara Koz Paley, Adele Riepe, Cathy Rodgers, Randy Sher Rubin, Charles Schwartz, and Edie Wiener.

Carole Hyatt

ACKNOWLEDGMENTS

For her assistance in the updating of this book, it is a pleasure to thank Connie DeSwann who has collaborated with me on many projects. She is a consummate professional.

Thanks go to Betsy Brown, my editor who recognized the need for this updated version and has been a staunch ally at McGraw-Hill.

It is also a pleasure to thank Patricia Linden for her collaborative assistance in the original version of this book.

I owe a special debt to Linda Gottlieb, whose original thought it was to translate *The Woman's Selling Game Workshop* into a book. Her enthusiasm and original outline validated this project.

I am particularly indebted to my friend and colleague, Judith Gerberg, who assisted in the original research for the Workshop by becoming an Avon Lady, giving a Tupperware party, and taking lessons at Arthur Murray and Berlitz, to name a few of her exceptional activities. Her vivid descriptions of her experiences and her common-sense application of them aided the shaping of the material.

My appreciation goes to Burt Saltman for illuminating the examples of reality, communication, and affinity.

To my daughter Ariel, whom I admire greatly for her abilities not only as a suburb marketer but as a woman who brings substantive advice and integrity to her rapidly expanding client list, I say thanks.

To my husband Gordon I give a very special salute for his agreement, participation, and support for my every endeavor.

Richard Malavet, whose talents and participation extend far beyond the computer and fax machine, gets my special thanks.

Finally, it is with deep remembrance of two dear departed friends, my research partner June Esserman and designer stylist Cloud Rich, both of whose wise counsel is imbedded in every page of this book.

INTRODUCTION
WHY *THE WOMAN'S NEW SELLING GAME*

When *The Woman's Selling Game* was published in 1979, it was one of the first books on demystifying the "how-to" of careers. It stressed the fact that the basis of any career, whatever you choose, requires that you learn to *sell yourself or anything else.*

1979 was also an enormously interesting time for women. In the late 1970s, most women were still grappling with whether or not they believed in their right to excel on the job or their right to equal pay for equal work—but were unsure how far to take other issues involving the centuries-long disputes between men and women. Or they were feminists with a capital *"F,"* believing in the leveling of male domination socially, emotionally, professionally, and economically while promulgating true woman power. Or they were somewhere between these ideologies.

Work, most of all, became the platform for women's development and flowering. With their accomplishment in business came the nagging and seemingly unanswerable question: Is work a job or a career? Men, for the most part until then the money-earners upon whom the family relied for security, rarely asked this question out loud. Work was a necessity, hopefully made easier by promotions and raises—never mind the search for fulfillment.

The world changed dramatically between 1970 and 1979. The economy changed, sexual attitudes changed, the quest for money and acquisition became a more open and acceptable goal, divorce statistics escalated—and more women than ever entered the work force. Many women—single, divorced, or married—discovered their skills and ambition on the job. They wanted to move up in a company or start their own businesses. But since it was 1979, many women had no idea where to begin.

I was a rarity at the time—a woman entrepreneur and co-founder of a successful market research company, Hyatt Esserman Research, Inc. I knew I wanted to help other women and teach them what I had learned from able and brilliant male mentors as well as from my own experience at my company.

The idea for *The Woman's Selling Game* evolved out of a course I taught at one of the first schools dedicated to fostering women's skills, the Woman's School. My course was called, "How to Run Your Own Business," which appealed to many women who wanted to follow this path. My students had wonderful ideas as to the kinds of businesses they wanted to run and looked to me for information about being an entrepreneur. I felt some ingredient was missing from the course, though—some basic skill I couldn't put my finger on. I wasn't sure what it was until one woman raised her hand and said, "All this information is great. What I need now is someone to go out and sell for me."

I stopped the course right there and said, "Aha! This is it. This is what women are missing about running a successful business: *selling themselves and selling their product.*"

I went on to interview hundreds of women, asking them their opinions on selling. The questions I asked them included why they did or didn't want to sell themselves (or a product), what they thought negotiation really meant, and what their problems were with asking for money for themselves and getting contracts. Out of this research I developed a seminar, and from the seminar a book, *The Woman's Selling Game.*

THEN AND NOW: WHAT YOU MUST KNOW

Consider these realities: downsizing, consultancies, freelancing, by-project work, outsourcing, the ten-job resume, the entrepreneurial spirit. These are the trends you'll find in the marketplace today and they have changed the nature of what we once called "job security." As corporations merge and become restructured, your chances of staying at one company and retiring after 25 years with them are very slim. You will more likely have four to six career changes and multiple jobs, and many of us will work project-by-project at one company or more.

One career or six, what really matters is how you sell yourself and anything else—to nab the promotion, close the sale and get the account, ask for a raise, develop creatively and see the fruits of your work. *The basis for all this is the ability to sell.*

THINGS THAT HAVE REMAINED THE SAME

In working on the revision of this book, I found a few notable changes both in the nature of the marketplace and in how you'll need to work to do your best in sales into the twenty-first century. These changes coexist with what I found to be *unchanged* for women over the years:

- mixed messages,
- attitudes, and
- the "glass slipper."

THE PREVALENCE OF MIXED MESSAGES

There are many conflicts resulting from mixed messages. Parents may have said to their daughters, "It's good to work," but in the next breath they've said, "... and it's a good thing to stay at home."

Over the past several decades, many women watched as their mothers left the home, got jobs, and achieved. Such women may have been proud of their mothers, but so did they resent their not "being there for me." Part of the problem is the brutality of finances—many women had to work to maintain a decent lifestyle, often only possible for a family with two incomes.

Daughters of women who fought to work in the 1960s and 70s are now looking at their options. Some feel entitled to get ahead faster; others seem fearful. Others want a different kind of life, not a life whose focus is achievement. My daughter Ariel, who's in her mid-20s, recently said to me, "I don't want to work the way you worked. I want a more balanced life." But since she's an owner of a company that promotes rock groups, she's working as hard as I ever worked, if not harder, to make her mark. But that can change.

ATTITUDES

Mixed messages are the source of another key career issue: Women are still afraid to *ask for* what they want. They may have command of the language of negotiation—and there may be more social acceptance of women asserting themselves to make the asking easier—but underneath, there is still that nagging doubt. Women ask themselves, "Do I really deserve this raise?" Or, resenting the very question, they say, "Why do I have to *ask* for money? Why can't they just *give* it to me? I work hard, don't I?" Or, they wonder if having a lot of money and being successful will diminish their femininity.

Not asking for what they want, then, keeps them on a plateau where they're always striving toward something they think they *can't* have, something that's just up there on the next plateau. Why do we have such difficulty in asking for ourselves? Simply put, there is a mistaken subconscious connection between asking/getting and being feminine. That is, if we're selling, we're not being "nice" girls.

Asking/getting connects to other psychological issues, too. There is the fear of success (worry about whether we can handle the added responsibility and gain the respect of others), its flip side, the fear of failure (doubt that we're worthy of success, anxiety that we'll lose the position of power and be humiliated), and fear of rejection (worry about others' opinions of us and our worth).

The simple fact is that you must *ask for what you want and what you are worth.* No one will do it for you. This is not being "pushy," but a good career strategy. Since sexual discrimination is still alive and well and a major, if cleverly hidden, aspect of promotion policy in many companies, you must ask for your price, plus some. Remember, women still earn less than men for the same job. Do your best to change those statistics. You'll find tips on asking and getting throughout this book.

THE "GLASS SLIPPER"

Women are still falling into the trap of wearing the "glass slipper," that is, aspiring to "staff" jobs rather than *line* jobs. Women still feel that staff jobs fit better and look better on them—we're attracted to jobs that are peripheral to producing and distributing the product and to the work done at the company. Human resources, legal, publicity, and secretarial are all staff positions and the first to be cut when a company is downsized. These kinds of skills can be outsourced—contracted by the project as needed. If you work for a company and hold one of these kinds of jobs, expand your knowledge so you can sell yourself and move into the line, the basis of the business, and its fundamental workings.

Wear a glass slipper and you may hit the glass ceiling—that is, achieve only so much and then look up to see the guys in control. As of this writing, there's only one woman CEO of a Fortune 500 company in the United States. If we look at government jobs, there are about the same number of women in power positions in the late 1990s as there were in the 1980s.

One of the early goals of the women's movement was to put women into the power pipeline. The problem is that the pipeline sprang a leak because women got stuck in staff jobs and didn't sell themselves *into the line*—where the real business is conducted. We're still waiting around to be invited into every aspect of business and still hesitant to ask for what we really want to get from the pipeline. All this requires an ability to sell.

THINGS THAT HAVE CHANGED

The following are some important changes that have occurred since 1979—trends for you to be aware of as you go through this book:

- technology,
- time,
- money,
- power of women in the workforce,
- global competition, and
- network marketing.

TECHNOLOGY

When *The Woman's Selling Game* was first published, the electric typewriter, the file cabinet, and the calculator were three office staples without which no business could run. Now their functions can be programmed into one machine: the personal computer. Bill Gates and Steve Jobs not only changed the world's perception of technology in the 1980s, but they made it user friendly.

Apply for a job today, and you will almost surely be expected to know or learn how to use the software the company is using. Millions of people have daily access to or familiarity with a personal computer and a software program or two. Many people also carry a portable PC "notebook" the size of a small bound book that's a phone directory, calendar, word processor, checkbook balancer, and source of spreadsheets, all in one. Beyond the PC, there are E-mail, the Internet, and the cellular phone, all sources of communication and information that are necessary for business—and successful sales.

To sell yourself now, you must plug in to the new technologies.

TIME

Our sense of time has changed remarkably since the 1970s. Now we are all "time poor." Once you could have taken 15 minutes of a meeting to introduce yourself and chat to break the ice. Now this luxury is no longer feasible, nor is it acceptable. To make your sale, you must move gracefully from a minute or two of hand shaking right into your pitch.

MONEY

What you could purchase for $150 in 1979 and what that amount can purchase today are vastly different. In 1979, getting paid $150 a day was considered good money, while $1,500 a day put you in a special category—super model or super mogul. Today, the freelance consultant asking $1,500 a day is in the ballpark, not in a league of her own.

Know what you're worth in today's market and ask for it. This book will tell you how.

THE INCREASING POWER OF WOMEN IN THE WORKFORCE

Understand just how much a part of this vast market you are: According to the Women's Bureau at the U.S. Department of Labor, more women than ever are entering the workforce. The latest numbers reveal that women represent about 46 percent of the labor force—that's 57 million women—and that percentage is expected to increase to 48 percent by 2005. Of the approximately 67 million families in the country, 18 percent—averaging out racial and regional differences—are maintained by women. But women are earning only 72 percent of what men earn for the same job.

GLOBAL COMPETITION

With super stores, super corporations, international trade, buy-outs and buy-ins all common features, you need to stand out by finding your niche—and selling it tactically. For example, if you open a boutique that sells women's sportswear, what makes your shop different? Why would customers come to you instead of, say, a discounter like Loehmann's or a large chain store like Wal-Mart or Sears?

In these times, good selling means you must differentiate yourself from the others in a vast and expanding market. Are you offering better service, greater quality for a reasonable price, smarter styling, faster delivery? Even if you work for a company and are not literally an entrepreneur, think in terms of specialization—your niche—and what you can offer to make you different in this golden age of marketing.

THE ACCEPTANCE OF **NETWORK MARKETING** AS A FULL-TIME OR PARALLEL CAREER CHOICE

Since many of us will be in and out of multiple jobs during our working lives, we could all benefit from a safety net. One way to fortify your net is to rediscover network marketing, once known as "multilevel marketing." In the 1980s, it suffered from a tarnished reputation as pyramid schemes tantalized too many people more interested in greed than in building a business.

The industry has been pretty much cleaned up, and enduring companies like Mary Kay and Shaklee have shown why it is now earning billions of dollars: Network marketing is simply a good thing to fall back on and works well as a parallel career—a way of earning extra money. Here is an arena where you may learn to be a superstar in sales; Chap. 11 will outline how.

I hope that *The Woman's **New** Selling Game* will help you strategize to get what you want. This book has time-tested concepts and exercises that will teach you the skills to achieve what should be yours. Once you make the sales techniques second nature, the game will be yours!

WHAT SELLING IS

The essence of selling is simply this: finding out what somebody needs and providing it.

Read the axiom again. Clearly, selling is a woman's game. Nearly every woman has been programmed from childhood to serve others, to please, to be a giver in a world of users and givers.

Since selling is all about thinking of what the other person needs rather than about your own desires and problems, the question is, why is your sales ability not automatically terrific? What has kept you from perfecting the business techniques men seem to have been born with, the techniques that are essential to success?

Numbers tell us that women constitute 46 percent of the U.S. workforce, yet only 10 percent of those women hold top executive positions and, of that 10 percent, a mere 6 percent are in middle management. Even more significant is the disparity between men's and women's earning power. In the professional and technical fields, women are being paid 25 percent less than men, and in sales they earn less than half what their male counterparts command. The time has come to repair these inequities by providing women with the selling skills that traditionally have been men's purview.

This book is designed to equip you with the tools and ammunition you need to give you that selling edge, to let you achieve measurably better results in everything you do. Having these power tools at your command will take the guesswork, fear, and mystery out of selling, and will enable you to succeed by giving you control over what you are doing.

I had a great job for ten years in a corporation I thought would last forever. I watched my friends being downsized in other places and felt lucky to be here, at the company that was as stable as the Rock of Gibraltar. Last year, things changed. Top management came in and disbanded my entire department—and I was out on my behind. Now I have to start all over again in a different business world. I hate the idea of feeling like I'm a prostitute—going out and selling myself over and over for the next job.

The company should have known what my worth was and kept me on. I was loyal to them, wasn't I?

Last year I raised $728,000 by writing grant proposals, organizing door-to-door canvassing teams, and producing brilliantly conceived brochures. The foundation I work for is thrilled beyond belief. Yet I still haven't been able to get up enough gumption to ask for the raise that is certainly due me. When it comes to getting money for somebody else, I'm marvelous. When it's for me, I'm a total washout.

I had some photographs I wanted to sell to a gallery and I called up and asked for an appointment to bring them in. She said, "Well, we have plenty of photos on hand and I'm not sure what the buying situation is. I don't think it's good to see you right now. Call back in a couple of weeks and we'll talk about it then." I said, "Okay, I'll call you back," but I never did. I took her putting me off as a judgment—that I wasn't any good and she wouldn't want my photographs anyway so I might as well go on to something else. I translated it into avoiding confronting her and selling her something.

I've been in audiovisual "how-to" publishing for about 18 years and am toying around with the idea of striking out on my own. But I don't know how to present myself, how to get my points across, how to clinch a deal, or how to talk on the telephone. I'm not a natural salesperson. I don't have the knowledge or confidence to get up and do it.

THE BRIGHTEST IDEAS ARE USELESS UNLESS YOU CAN SELL THEM

If you are like most women, it's a pretty safe bet that you are missing the one business skill that will help you climb to the top of your field. Nobody ever told you how important it really is, and because you lack that information, you are being held back—nibbling at little slices when you could have the whole cheese. What's missing is the ability to sell yourself, your product, your service, or your talent. Until you develop that skill, no matter how expert you are or become, you're in danger of being forever stalled on your road to success.

Whether you are an actor, designer, public relations pro, secretary, teacher, doctor of psychology, or volunteer worker, you are as certainly in the business of selling as if you were in a more obviously sales-oriented business: a real estate agent, a manufacturer's rep, stockbroker, boutique owner, or car dealer. The fact is inescapable, a simple truth. Face this reality: Before you can do whatever it is you do, you have to sell yourself, your idea, your product, your service, or your talent. Somebody has to buy what it is you do or it may as well not exist. It's like the woman at a party who waits for a man to come talk to her or to ask her to dance. She is decorative, novel, and really quite interesting. So is the painting on the wall.

THE FOUR KINDS OF CAREERS AND THE ONE THING THAT MAKES THEM: SELLING

There are four clear-cut situations in which you're going to need complete command of selling skills. As you read on, you will learn how to handle each type as it arises.

1. You will be selling when **the product is you.** At some points and in various guises, you are probably going to be looking for a means to advance your career through a job, a raise, or a promotion. What you'll be doing then is convincing people that they need you, that it will be to their advantage to use and reward you for helping them succeed. You'll be asking for what you want, and the way you will get it will be through your ability to sell yourself.

2. You will be selling **a product.** When your career involves selling tangible items—clothing, real estate, art, machinery, software,

or supplies of any nature—your mission will be to move the items from one place to another at a monetary profit. You will have to do this by convincing people that your product is superior to others, and that buying your product will be beneficial.

3. You will be selling **a service.** When you have an intangible product to move, yours or someone else's service, you will need to know how to persuade people that that particular service will improve their lives in some way. You may be an adviser, consultant, teacher, or artisan, a service provider or an agent for somebody else. It's all the same. To get people to use the service, you will have to know how to sell it.

4. You will be selling **a talent.** If you are a writer, artist, actor, director, or designer—in any pursuit whose aim is to express an innate gift—that expression will be complete only when you have given life to your talent by moving it out of the studio or office and into the marketplace. Persuading people to buy your talent requires the same skills as persuading people to buy your product, your service, or yourself: the techniques and strategies of selling.

You still say you're not in the business of selling? That's what I said, too, when I got my first job in television. Having sailed into a CBS television station on a platform of little more than a headful of workable program ideas, I was convinced it was strictly my ability to churn out ideas that had sold the station manager on hiring me. Even after an incident that had me accompanying the sales crew on a client pitch to help explain one of my program ideas, I failed to catch on—I still thought the client had bought solely because the idea was a good one. It wasn't until much later, when I was sitting on the other side of the table at CBS, buying other people's program concepts, that I realized what was really going on.

My revelation sprang from a week when four different people came in, each with an almost identical idea. That's not unusual in itself; you know how ideas often circle the atmosphere, ripe to be plucked. This one was good, and after hearing the same theme four times, I bought it from one of the four presenters. Then I began to think: "Something intriguing has taken place here." Since there was no substantial difference between any of the four ideas, why did I choose one of them in particular? I mulled the question seriously, and when the answer finally registered, it was this: My purchase decision was based not solely on the idea, but on the person who'd sold it to me. It had been somebody who inspired confidence, who was able to communicate well and get me to agree, who persisted when I exhibited reluctance, who was willing to work with me and give me a chance to add my own ideas to the package. In short, someone who sold me.

What became evident to me was that it's not enough just to have ideas—anybody can do that and there isn't a truly new one under the sun anyway. Clearly, if an idea is going to survive, you have to have the ability to sell it. I became conscious of something about myself too: My greatest strength wasn't generating ideas, it was the ability to sell the ideas. And I didn't have to be ashamed of it. Before, when I thought of "selling," a little piece of me thought of it as most women do: with its dirty connotations of pushiness, deception, trickiness, and aggression. I was mistaken.

WORDS CAN HOLD YOU BACK

What selling really means is finding out what others want and then helping them get it. It is convincing others to want what you can provide; getting them to buy what you have so that you will all benefit as a result. Selling is success, and success is when everybody wins.

Yet selling and success are words that can be abhorrent. They do not sit well. Their ill-repute goes back to the antediluvian convention that most of our mothers were brought up on and that seeped down to us: Girls who are nice do not display social traits that show worldly ambitions. Instead, they are "sugar and spice." It's a cotton-candy convention spun of air and little substance, and it loads the two words with some very nasty and unfeminine connotations. The implications of pushiness, deceit, and unflattering maleness overwhelm and defeat us before we begin. They make successful selling seem unladylike at best and immoral at worst.

Many women still operate from a mentality of deprivation, scarcity, or poverty. At the extreme, this is the "bag lady" syndrome, fear of losing everything, including the ability to take care of ourselves. I find that some women are afraid to give so that they can get something back. They worry about being generous, more concerned with hanging on to what they have, sure the universe will limit what they get. In the scarcity mode, women think, "It's a mistake I got this contract" or "It's a mistake I'm being paid this amount" and "What if I make a mistake and lose it?"

Part of the nice-girl thinking is the very career-busting idea of *limitation.* For many women, the sense of scarcity, giving, and getting in business is directly related to the giving and getting of love. That is, there are limits to love, to what you think you can get out of life—and that includes money and career. It probably develops from a fear of being hurt, or of loss—What if you give love and don't get it back? What if the person we love makes us feel beholden with every bite of food? Will you never give again? Can you trust another again? If not, then we think, "I have limits!" or "What the world will provide is very limited and I will be on the short end of the stick."

Some of us have inherited these kinds of nonproductive and stultifying messages that we keep in the backs of our minds—and they stop us from succeeding. This is because many women transfer their feelings about love to work.

The response that makes a grown woman say, "Ugh, selling is pushy and dirty and it's not for me," comes straight out of these kind of programmed reflexes inculcated in most of us during girlhood. We learned to play with dolls, paste movie stars into scrapbooks, stir fudge in the kitchen, and not make waves ... while our brothers were on the baseball and football fields learning to sharpen their sales and bargaining abilities. Remember how you always got approval for being passive, undemanding, agreeable—and how the guys in the gang were rewarded every time they spoke up, made trades and deals, used somebody else's strength to help make themselves or the team look better? "Stay in the dollhouse and be still, little girl. Never mind what the big boys are up to."

Society's attitudes have changed, and the last three generations of women reflect these changes. There are "generation X-ers" coming up now, who grew up with many channels open to them, the first waves of obstacles having been broken down by previous generations of women. They are known by their greater sense of entitlement and their slightly cynical edge about life. There are the 35- to 45-year-olds, many of whom have battle scars, have started their own businesses, and are still fighters. And there is the older generation of working women, 45 and up, some of whom still hold on to the old ideals about womanhood impeding their career progress. Of course, there are cross-generational influences and character types—you pick up attitudes and inspiration from others, from the trends and opportunities in your time, and from experience.

Nevertheless, many of us remain stuck in the attitudes we were brought up on, and it's no wonder we think selling and succeeding are guilt-edged synonyms for taking advantage of other people's weaknesses, being false, and acting unethically. We never had a chance to latch onto the reality, which is this: The only people—men or women—who act unethically are those who believe it is acceptable to lie, cheat, steal, and mislead others. If that is not your standard, you don't have to worry about the ethics of selling; immorality is not your style. If you are an ethical person to begin with and you are selling, by nature your concentration will be on ethical behavior: filling someone else's needs, providing real benefits, doing something nice by helping.

I think you'll agree that the time has come to clean up our mental vocabularies, destroy the stifling myths, and get rid of the negative, unrealistic notions that still lurk in the backs of our minds and hold us back.

DEBUNKING THE MYTHS

Attitudes create labels, and vice versa. Somebody can call your new pink dress "chic" and you'll feel good about wearing it, or "dorky" and you'll doubt your choice. In the same way, people have developed attitudes and labels about men and women. Consider these stereotypes and the effects false labels impose. Knowing that the labels traditionally attached to women are merely societal myths can be the "Ah-ha" experience that releases you from fear and activates the real abilities you've possessed all along.

The Antisemantics of Sexist Mythology

He asserts.	She's pushy.
He's well-traveled.	She's been around.
He's under a lot of pressure.	She's out of control/getting her period.
He's considering the idea.	She's indecisive.
He's highly organized.	She's compulsive/obsessed/impossible to please.
He's powerful.	She's controlling/castrating.

SELLING IS A WOMAN'S GAME

To sell successfully is to utilize the life skills you are already well-versed in by transferring what you know from one environment to another. To put it another way: If you were to write your autobiography and translate what I call emotional words into career phraseology, you'd find that what you do every day is sell people—your husband, your lover, your parents, your children, anybody you think may need what you've got. Selling people is just another way of saying helping; it's a matter of changing the language in your head.

MANIPULATION: THE LOADED WORD THAT'S OKAY

New language notwithstanding, here's a line that is usually a shocker: Selling is a process that is manipulative, and you are undoubtedly one of the top manipulators of all time.

Does the word need laundering for you? Let's take it apart and examine what manipulation really means. According to Webster, the word means "to manage or utilize skillfully." In selling, that means shaping people's behavior through skillful negotiation, persuasion, control, influence, enlightenment, and persistence. It's the same thing psychiatrists do—at $150 a throw. They shape their patients' behavior and when their manipulative shrinkage works out well, we see it as a good thing. Likewise, when you shape your children's behavior, guide them to do what's beneficial for them, you're manipulating and you're doing a good thing. So why do we hear the word as evil? Why is it that what we do at home to shape behavior is benign and desirable, but the minute we make the same effort away from home turf, we worry that it's aggressive and pushy rather than assertive and helpful? Performances at home and at somebody's office are not, it seems, equal. Not if you're clinging to yesterday's fairy tales, that is.

THE BEAUTIFUL AND THE DAMNED

Fairy tales taught us to believe in a few impossibly outdated ideas that sounded reasonable when we were seven or eight years old. The stories always went the same way: There was the king, the queen, the princess, the handsome, courageous young suitor, and the evil-doer. In the story, the king has a problem he cannot solve. The problem becomes so acute that he puts up his treasure, his kingdom, and his daughter as ransom. Whoever will take care of the problem can have all three. The queen, of course, doesn't speak up—even if she's got the answer—but remains behind the throne where queens belong. This leaves an opportunity open for the clever young man who is about to happen upon fate: a problem, a castle, a bounty.

He solves the problem, gets the treasure (the money), the kingdom (real estate), and the princess (the silent pawn who will provide him with children). When the king and queen die, the young man and his bride take over the throne. He now wields the power and the new queen settles down behind the throne, like her mother before her, and is never heard of again. The moral: Good men are brave and powerful, good women are pretty, passive rewards.

Once in a while the story changes and there's a stepmother in the picture. Staying behind the throne is not for this woman because she is wicked—in fact, she may have done in the king with a tasty last meal, insuring her power. She's fearless, throwing her weight around, threatening his children, demanding her due. Everybody fears and hates her and in the end she winds up dead, having undone herself. So that's the second moral: Women who act for their own ends are terrible, period.

It's no wonder, with all those fairy tales drummed into our brains—some with mixed messages—that we're still afraid to go after what we want. We might get it. There is still the fear that with success, others will resent us, threaten us; we'll lose control of our reason with the smallest amount of power and others will offer us feasts of poisoned apples!

THE FEAR OF SUCCESS

Fear is the reason people avoid success—fear of what success will do to their lives, fear of not being able to succeed, fear of too much success, and just fear in general. The nice thing about fear, though, is that it's universal. Everyone has fears, and everyone has fears related to career achievement.

Reality: *Success is scary, and so what?*

I'm a 33-year-old dress designer with 12 years of experience. Four years ago I was going great guns, right at the edge of spectacular success. Just as I was about to sign my biggest contract, I mysteriously got sick and literally had to drop out of the scene.

I'm just now putting myself back together, and looking back on those four years I can see now why I dropped out. I was afraid of the success that was coming. I was scared to go ahead because then I would have responsibilities. I would have to take care of people. I'd be in what I saw as a man's role and wouldn't be feminine anymore. No one would want to take care of me, ever.

I would get into a money crunch—meeting overhead, making profits, that kind of thing. I wouldn't meet successful men because men don't want women who might be more successful than they. I'd be working all the time and have no room left for a love or a family. It seemed as if I would have no choices left and would never be able to do anything else but work at being successful. I was afraid I was surrendering options, giving up choices.

Now that I'm back in the market and starting my own business again, I realize that I don't have to give up anything to be successful. I can have it all: love, a family, everything I want. Success really can be a way of expanding my life—it doesn't mean shrinking back and giving up choices.

GET YOUR FEAR OUT OF THE CLOSET

Let's face this anxiety and get rid of one of the biggest, scariest barriers you face—the fear you'll be rejected for looking pushy—and its consequence, that you fear success. It's what keeps many a woman hesitating at the edge, so scared she'll lose something she won't leap in and start winning. Even though being afraid to succeed is common among women (and many men) and that puts you in good company, if you are afraid of success it's a sure bet you're not going to get it.

No fear I know of just vanishes. You have to tackle it as a reality. Acknowledge that it is there and get on with what it is you want to do. Handle fear the way you handle a car when you hit a slick spot. What you do is to go into the skid rather than try to fight what is happening. You act according to what is actually going on, collecting information, keeping your eyes wide open to the real possibilities of the situation, and coping with the facts rather than conjuring up Cassandra's fantasies.

I'll give you a good example of how this works. You've been called upon to speak before a group for the first time in your life. You're scared to death and shaking like a leaf. Instead of standing there shaking, acknowledge that you're scared. Tell the audience, "This is the first time I've ever spoken before a large group and I'm so scared I'm shaking." There. The facts are out, nobody hates you, and you no longer have to fight to conceal your fear from the audience.

It helps to know that you are not alone and I will tell you that everybody in the world is scared at some point. Novices, pros, men, women—everyone is scared to one degree or another and the fear never goes away completely. How you choose to feel about fear and what you do with the feelings, of course, are what really matter. A certain amount of apprehension can work in your favor and keep you alert, on your toes, and buzzing with adrenalin—rather like a sprinter at the Olympics, poised on the block, waiting for the starting gun, or an actor about to face the footlights and speak her first line on stage. Such is the kind of "fear" that makes you feel alive and makes you perform at your best.

Take your fear along with you and work with it, not against it. The humanist Stewart Emery says, "The world is divided into two kinds of people: the people who are fearful and can't move ahead and the people who are fearful and take their fear with them." For a perfect example of Emery's second kind of person, look at Katharine Hepburn. She has said, "I am terrified of cameras." Having acknowledged her terror, she took it along with her and went on to perform brilliantly, and later on in interviews to tell people, unabashedly, that what she had more than anything was "charisma" and something that looked good on the screen.

WHY YOU'RE AFRAID IN THE FIRST PLACE

Now let's take a look at your "skids" and work with them one at a time in this mini-crash-course on your "inner career woman." These are: your fear of success, fear of failure, and fear of rejection.

FEAR OF SUCCESS.   Studies in the psychology of women, particularly those 45 and over, conclude that our archetypical purpose and function is to be subordinate, to serve and to please others. The grand scenario still calls for the males of the world to be the users, the females the givers. We are brought up to seek happiness in serving those to whom we are most attached emotionally, usually a man: father, husband, or lover. By the same token, it is inherent in our social conditioning that men be the dominant actors; the implicitly superior race cast as leaders, rulers, managers, directors; the bold ones, the autocrats of the breakfast and conference tables. The successes.

Each race, the dominant (male) and the subservient (we, the female), has its own fears and prejudices as a result of this scenario. The Dominants don't want to give in to the Subordinates, and we Subservients are afraid of the Dominants because we think they must know something we don't. Since the whole business is a fantasy based on an assumption of director versus servant, the myth and its mysteries perpetuate themselves in an endless cycle. The supportive little-woman image has been cast in bronze.

This, then, is the tradition many women come to maturity with: Socially and professionally we are programmed to think of ourselves as unequals. We are groomed to serve, support, depend, act for the good of others and not—perish the notion—for the good of ourselves. Even today we glibly say, "This is not us," but it *is* us, acting out the messages our mothers gave us.

What happens? We may succeed at a career and sabotage it. Or we may succeed at a career but feel guilty or uneasy about it, *until we don't*. In a recent interview, singer Carly Simon said that when she was married to singer James Taylor in the 1970s, they both had hit records out at the same time—but hers, "You're So Vain," went to number one while his hovered around number ten. She not only felt badly about besting her husband, a respected performer, on the charts, she publicly defended his song as "better." Twenty years later, she found herself making the *same* statement about the songs, then stopped herself, and with a little laugh, realized what she was doing.

FEAR OF FAILURE.   Very simply, there are three bases for a fear of failure: loss of ego, loss of status, or loss of money. Women with a fear of failure, I've found, show it in two classic ways—those who act and those who don't.

Here's a typical case: Perhaps, you've been promoted twice on the job, then suddenly you're passed over for a big promotion that you and those around you expected would be yours. Although you've still got a job, you feel hurt—you have a bruised ego and a sense of humiliation because of a perceived loss of status. Two down, you feel, and possibly the threat of a third on the way. You may interpret the situation—the missed promotion—as an indication of having failed. In truth, this is a career setback, not failure!

Conversely, there's the woman so held captive by a fear of failure that she never acts to do what's required to accomplish anything at all.

FEAR OF REJECTION.   I once met a woman after one of my seminars who told me that she'd been working as a manager of an upscale boutique for 15 years, really running the show, but getting no recognition. Ruth combed the want ads for a better job worthy of her managerial skills, wrote her cover letters and resumes, but could not get herself to send them out. Ruth's problem? Fear of rejection, or a fear of how others will judge her as a person. She's confused and hasn't disconnected the two—who she is at the core and what she's selling in the job market, or how potential employers will judge her for her skills.

While fear of failure has a basis in losing something, fear of rejection has its roots in *wanting* something you dread others will not give you. Ruth cannot take the first step out, but there are other women who *can* go on the interviews but interpret a comment from a potential employer like, "You're not right for the job here" as "You're not good enough."

Don't take turn-downs personally or take them as a judgment that you're unworthy. You are not offering yourself or your soul up for the job, but a set of skills.

REVOLUTION ON THE HOME FRONT

Came the decade of female emancipation and, with it, difficulties, ambivalence, and turmoil. The heretofore stereotypical girl-woman pursues a career. She is good at it, a winner. She succeeds by focusing on her own needs and desires. She is "selfish," "aggressive." She makes decisions, influences other people, gains recognition, becomes financially and socially independent. Suddenly the world is upended. All the old conditioning is turned around. The status quo is upset and, like it or not, so are she and her beloved. Neither sees that all her experience in managing a household, rearing and guiding the children, reading and reacting to the signals men give out has translated directly into selling experience. They see her career success as something that changes the balance, alters the ground rule that says she exists to serve him, not herself or others.

It threatens them both. He fears losing the emotional, social, and financial dominance he is accustomed to enjoying. She fears that her success will rock their boat too hard and he will abandon her. Abandonment is a scary prospect. Nobody tolerates it well. It's no wonder that women who do not understand what is happening today, who have not intimately studied how women's roles have changed, suffer from the fear of success. Many women earning more money than their husbands suffer from the same fears deep down.

You, me, all of us have been set up with every answer in the book as to why we should not succeed fully. Recognizing what the realities are all about is the factor that enables us to grow as individuals, and to succeed.

THE POWER AND THE THRONE

If you are going to proceed onward and upward in your career, you want to feel comfortable about emerging from being the invisible supporter behind the throne. You have to be willing to sit on the throne yourself, to be in the seat of power. You have to take the risk, if that's what it is for you, of focusing on yourself, of controlling your own life for your own purposes, of letting go of that programming that says self-fulfillment is a bad thing. It is the only way you will get from here to there.

Here is another useful translation for your career lexicon. Sitting on the throne where the power is does not mean that you are "tough" or "pushy." The terms imply that ambition and tenacity are male qualities and that you are gender-bending and overreaching your possibilities as a woman.

There will always be people who resent (or fear) your career plans, your vision for the future, or even your verbalized and as yet unfulfilled goals. Calling you "tough" means they acknowledge your power—and don't like it! So remember the new language in your autobiography: Change tough or pushy (or any other slangy word meant to short-circuit you) to *flexible* and continue on your road, extending your experience as a woman in control and able to bend with circumstances and win. That is the reality, and recognizing reality is the key to success in everything you do.

Recognize and take advantage of the network of collaboration and support that women are offering one another today. While men often take a stoic stance and refuse to acknowledge their fears about work and competition, women are sharing these emotions quite openly. This book contains many statements from women who were willing to share their ideas, attitudes, fears, and knowledge with other women. It is, in book form, the kind of support system that helps us all to grow.

UNCOVERING YOUR HIDDEN AGENDA

A long time ago, J. Pierpont Morgan made this perceptive observation: "A man generally has two reasons for doing a thing: one that sounds good, and the real one."

It's important to know the real reason you want to succeed, to be clear about what it is that motivates you most. Is your basic desire to gain money, approval, power, social contacts? Is there more than one moving force behind your wish for accomplishment? It's all right, whatever your answer, whatever it is you're looking for—as long as you are realistic about it. Often people tell themselves they're motivated by one thing—money, altruism, whatever they think sounds right—when they really are looking for something else. That something else is their hidden agenda, and a hidden agenda never really stays hidden. It will always emerge and take over.

You must be sure you are clear about the real reason for what you are doing. If you're out there selling and are working on a hidden agenda, it's going to get in your way. In the long run, if you keep on kidding yourself with inaccurate terms, it will prevent you from judging your progress realistically. More immediately and concretely, you'll wind up collecting something other than what you claim you're after. If you tell yourself the desire for money is what impels you, when your real goal is to meet men, that masked agenda will interfere with the results.

Recognizing your real motivation is not always easy; you may have to dig hard to discover it. I know, because the business of a hidden agenda was troublesome to me when I first began my career. I wanted to be in the theater, and in order to do so I had to sell theatrical packages to people connected with summer tents, schools, and civic auditoriums. At that point, I knew nothing about selling; I just knew that people had to buy my packages if I wanted to direct. So a lot of time and energy went into contacting people, using the techniques I'd learned in the dating process: get around, meet new men, charm them. Unconsciously, I was relying on personal appeal rather than on the benefits of the product I was offering. Without admitting it, I was really still looking for social contacts, and that's exactly what I got. I'd go into conference after conference, and come out with proposition after proposition—but never a contract. Despite what I told myself, social contacts were my primary motivation and business was number two on the agenda. The primary motivation won each time.

This went on for months, until I thought, "This is crazy. I'm supposed to be in there to sell a product because I want the money. I'm not getting the money because I'm just kidding myself about it. What I really want is dates and that's what I'm really getting. Since what I'm doing isn't working, I'd better start telling people what a good director and producer I am, instead."

Still not clear about why I was selling, I swung into an Oh-boy-look-at-me phase: "Here are all the wonderful things I've done. Please like my packages." I was looking for approval more than I was looking for business, and approval is what I got. There were tons of invitations to parties, choruses of how great Carole is, how nice, and how terrific. That didn't do much more for the bank balance than the propositions had; I hadn't figured out that what I had to do was learn what people needed and fit my product to their needs. I kept on collecting approval and no contracts, and it took a long time to finally force myself to reckon with the realities of what I was doing, so I could move on to concentrating on money as the prime motivator.

There's a surefire way of knowing if you are working on a hidden agenda: The universe will tell you so. If you keep on collecting something other than what you claim it is you're after, even though you sincerely believe your own claim, you can be sure it's because you're sending out messages that reflect the reality of your agenda.

There is no moral judgment to be made about real and hidden agendas. If dates rather than money are what you're really after, that's perfectly fine. The problem arises when you deceive yourself with false claims. Recognizing genuine motivations will bring genuine results.

STOP WHINING AND START WINNING

Kidding yourself with smoke screens and blue sky gets you nowhere, and bores everybody else. The copywriter at the ad agency who keeps telling everybody ad nauseam how she's going to write the great American novel because "creativity is the most important thing in my life" is a pain. She's not only a pain, she's sidetracking her career by not honestly concentrating on getting more of what she really wants: money.

Margaret is dazzlingly pretty, fairly intelligent—and a total fraud. She doesn't know she's a fraud, but the rest of the accounting firm where she works sees right through her. She went to work as a junior secretary to the firm's president five years ago and, through diligence, has worked her way up to being his assistant. Margaret is single, lives alone, and the office is her whole world. She waits on her boss like a slave. Nothing is too much. She brings his coffee in at ten on the dot, gets his shoes repaired and his suits pressed, works late nearly every night and frequently on weekends.

Sure, he takes advantage of her apparent willingness, and she cooperates with a smile. But outside the executive office it's another story. Margaret does nothing but bitch to her coworkers. She's a maid. She's overworked. The hours she keeps and the tasks she performs are inhuman. Everyone's wise to her story except Margaret, whose primary need is, after all, being fulfilled.

What she's after is the approval of her good-looking boss, her substitute for the love relationship she'd really like to have with him. By appearing to work very hard at being the perfect executive secretary, Margaret is able to conceal from herself what's really on her agenda. If only she'd stop bitching about it.

WHY I CAN'T DO WHAT I REALLY DON'T WANT TO DO

How many women have you heard complain that circumstances are against them? They can't get out and do what they want to do because they're housebound, husband-bound, child-bound, or bound to singlehood. In fact, they may not be bound by anything more than their own real, if hidden, wishes.

Take Elaine. When she was in her twenties she had a very successful career as an illustrator for shoe manufacturers. She married at 33 and proceeded to have the children she'd always yearned for. During her first few years at home, when the children were little, a number of her friends went back to work. Elaine began to gripe. She wanted to get back into the job market. She meant it, or thought she did, so she ran an ad for a housekeeper and interviewed them by the dozens. None were suitable. She tried. She'd hire one for a week or two, but something was always wrong. One housekeeper didn't get along with Elaine's daughter, another couldn't hit it off with her son. One fed the children junk food, another watched TV all day. The parade went on and on, while Elaine kept griping about how much she wanted to get back to work.

About a year after the parade began, the younger of the two children entered school and a miracle happened: The right housekeeper appeared. Or was she there all the time, hidden from Elaine who really wanted to stay home with her children?

Too bad Elaine hadn't faced the reality of her objectives in the first place. Staying home with the children was perfectly fine, if that's what she wanted to do until they were old enough for her to go back to work. It's failing to acknowledge real goals, and falling for false ones, that causes dissatisfied griping.

> **Reality:** *Other people can see your hidden agenda even if you've hidden it in a mental closet. You can take it out and see it any time.*

GET YOUR STORY STRAIGHT

It's easy to fall for your own story, as Margaret and Elaine have shown us. Alibis and rationales for doing anything but getting on goal and staying there are a dime a dozen. You've spun stories yourself, so admit it.

One good way to force yourself into acting on the realities is by role-playing. It's a technique we've used time and again in workshops and it works every time. What role-playing does is get you to voice and thereby to define what is really going on.

Dialogue will help you to clarify an issue, especially if you role-play together with a friend who's tuned in to what you are doing. Lacking a partner, try the technique all by yourself, switching from chair to chair if that helps you to get into the scene.

In this example of role-playing, there are two characters, the Positive Person and the Storyteller. You play the role of the Storyteller; if you have a hidden agenda, this is the role you play most of the time anyway. With your partner assuming the role of the Positive Person, here is how role-playing can help you get your story straight.

POSITIVE PERSON	STORYTELLER
I want to earn $10,000 more a year. To do that I have to complete my degree.	
	I can't complete the degree. My work keeps getting in the way. I have too big a workload now. I can't find time to get my house cleaned and finish my regular job. How can I find time to get the schoolwork done?
If I go back to school it will take me two years, taking two courses a semester, to complete my master's degree.	
	Besides, my apartment has to be painted and I need a new couch.
With my master's, I can apply for a specific job I've had my eye on within my own company. I need twenty more credits. Each credit is $500; $500 times twenty is $10,000. Therefore I need $10,000 plus two nights a week for the next two years.	

POSITIVE PERSON	STORYTELLER
	Ten thousand dollars! But I need a new couch. I have to have the apartment painted. And besides, there is no way I can unload the extra responsibilities that already take up two nights a week.
I could let the house go another two years. The paint job would be $1,000. Instead of buying a couch for $1,200, I could slipcover for $200. I'd have $2,000 to start.	
	Well, that part's all right, but I simply won't have the time. And you know how impossible the boss is. He's new and I have to keep teaching him his job. It takes a lot of time.
I spend a lot of time complaining about my boss. Since he arrived six months ago, he's taken up at least an hour a day of talking time and at least another hour of thinking time. That's ten hours a week. The ten hours a week I spend complaining about my boss I could spend in school.	
	I really like complaining about my boss. Every night over dinner, Harry and I chortle about his latest blunder.
I will keep the pleasure of talking about him over dinner with Harry, but talking over the phone to my friends has got to go.	
	OK, I'm convinced. I'll go back to school. I'll put it on my goal sheet as a two-year plan. But what about the rest of the money?
I know I have money for this semester. I'll enroll immediately. After I've enrolled I'll start applying for grants and scholarships. If they don't come through, I'll apply for a loan.	

This role-play, as with all role-playing done honestly, ended with the decision that was best—in this case, to return to school. It might have ended with the decision that the effort required to get a degree was not worth the pursuit.

If you cannot role-play, there are other ways to uncover your hidden agenda. As you do the exercises in Chap. 3, look carefully at your secondary choices; they may be indicative of your hidden agenda. Keep a diary or journal, taking special care to record your thoughts about your goals, and see if a hidden agenda emerges when you reread the journal. Career counseling is another excellent way to unmask a hidden agenda.

Ask your friends what they see as your hidden agenda. Really listen to the answers without defending yourself. We see our friends clearly and can identify their agendas with great accuracy. When it comes to turning the mirror on ourselves, we go blank.

Remember, there is nothing wrong with having a hidden agenda, only with failing to recognize its presence and unknowingly letting it hold you back from what you could be getting.

The best way to handle a hidden agenda is to unmask it, so you can deal from a reality base.

Reality: *Unless you are clear and honest about what you want, you are always going to feel gypped.*

SETTING GOALS

My ultimate business goal is to be in a supervisory role, making decisions that are to be implemented. I want to fit that in with a lot of money. Then I think I would like to change. I want to always be flexible enough so if I want to become a college instructor, I'll be loose enough to go after that.

I never want to feel I can't change my mind if I decide that I've accomplished X and want to switch careers and do something else. Right now I'd like to have enough money so I can have a big house in a good neighborhood and send my kids to the right schools. I'm figuring out a system for it and when I reach that plateau, I'll go on to the next one.

THE NEED TO KNOW YOUR GOAL

If you are going to go someplace, it's essential that you know where you are going. That may sound like belaboring the obvious. I'm sure it's a rare day that you seat-belt yourself into the car and drive off without having the dry cleaner, the supermarket, or some other definite place in mind. And when was the last time you bought a plane ticket to "somewhere"? When it comes to deciding on a career destination, however, it's often another story, a lot harder than putting "supermarket" on your list for the day.

Specificity as to where you're going in your career is something that needs to be consciously and thoughtfully arrived at. It's not an easy task. It takes laborious discipline to think things through clearly and definitely, and perceive clear-cut goals you can work toward. That labor is what separates the grumblers from the winners.

It's the people who haven't defined what it is they want who are always feeling cheated. The people who feel the satisfaction of having succeeded are the ones who have worked at something by reaching a specific goal.

Women's indecisiveness is hardly startling when one considers how little girls have been reared in our society. They've been taught—subtly or not so subtly—that they must wait. Until recently, they've waited for men to call them, waited for men to marry them, waited for men to define their lives for them. They've waited for men to set their goals. Even though women now call men up, stand up to them, compete with them for jobs and promotions, ultimately, we still think of ourselves in the handmaiden role. Somehow, most of us back down and give men the power.

As we approach the year 2000, the path with many forks still baffles women: One voice says, categorically, to take the path that is most hilly and hope it defines what you want; make your plan to get where you're going, and take the chance. Don't listen to the doomsayers. Step over the saboteurs. Think Madonna or Mary Kay and go for it! Another voice says that maybe women need to take the path of least resistance—to pull back and think like the 1940s or 1950s "woman behind the man." A number of bestselling books, like *The Rules,* suggest we revert to pre-sexual-revolution game-playing to "get the man," and pre-1960s waiting games to get the job.

Waiting is hardly the key to success in a career. This is something all little boys learn at an early age. Planning a career goal, like any other goal, is an action that requires conscious thought, hard labor, and perceptiveness. But that labor and willingness to open yourself to self-perceptions about goals are what separate the winners from the losers. Women who have failed to define what they want from life are the ones who are most likely to feel gypped. Those women who have discovered the value of having their own goals, as men have always done, are the ones who are getting what they want from life. The other women—the ones who want something from life but aren't sure what—fail to understand the process of goal-setting and, sadly, often fail to understand what it is that they have failed to do properly, why they aren't getting what they want.

Let me demonstrate what I mean in the way we illustrate it in workshop sessions. We use a crazy exercise there called "Puss in the Corner," a child's game, really. It's played with five people at a time. We mark off a square and have one person stand in the middle and each of the other four in a corner. The workshop leader calls out, "Puss in the Corner, one, two, three" and everybody has to change places. That's the only rule: They have to change places. We go through this silly exercise five times and then we ask, "Who feels she has won?" Session after session, the answers are the same. Half the people feel they've won, and the other half are flabbergasted that anybody would believe they've won anything in such a ludicrous game.

What happened with the "winners" is that they gave themselves specific goals. "I wanted to be in the middle and I got there," they tell us. Or "I wanted to try each space and I did." "I wanted to have a good time and I did." At this point the analogy becomes very clear to everybody. In life as in Puss in the Corner, when you make up your mind to get someplace specific and you succeed, you have won what you're after. When you have no plan, don't know what's going on and don't care, even if you luck out by reaching a "corner," you haven't the satisfaction of having won anything.

NOW THAT YOU'RE A GROWN-UP, WHAT DO YOU WANT TO BE?

> I knew when I was nine years old and helped put out the school newspaper that I had to be a writer. Everything I have done from that moment on has been for the purpose of becoming the best writer there is.

It is a wonderfully satisfying feeling to have a goal and achieve it. But not everybody is born knowing what it is he or she wants to go after. The woman who knew at age nine that she must become a writer is fortunate, as are all those who are blessed and driven by a creative talent. They have a ready-made affinity for something and can at least start with a broad direction. For many of us, with no particular affinity or immediately recognizable motivation, the basic question of how and where to even start presents a quandary. You may feel that you want to be doing *something,* but have no idea what it is that will fire the vital spark of enthusiasm that leads to success.

Some people who claim they have no talent have solved their quandary nonetheless, by thinking through what it is they already do well and with pleasure in their personal lives, then transferring that ability to business. One of the biggest social climbers I ever met at college went on to become a society columnist. A great matchmaker with a penchant for putting people together at parties uses her catalytic ability to match up business partners, for a fee. A brilliantly organized homemaker has made a successful business of organizing other people's closets; another terrifically talented caterer with a passion for tradition became the empire builder, Martha Stewart. Two of these women began their careers relatively late in life and with no previous business experience, wisely basing their ideas and goals on a transference of what they'd been doing as a matter of instinct.

YOU PROBABLY WON'T DO THIS AND YOU'RE CRAZY IF YOU DON'T

Here is an exercise that can help you to see what direction attracts you most. There'll be other exercises in this chapter that involve writing things down on paper, too. You probably will skip the writing part and generalize in your head instead. The best advice I can give you about really writing things down is to force yourself. The act of setting things down in writing will get you away from the vagueness we all tend to indulge in, and into being clear and specific about yourself.

This exercise is called "Paper in the Box." Each day for a month, write down on a piece of paper what it is you want to do that day. Don't stop to think about it. Anything that comes into your head is the right answer. Be outrageous, be practical—anything is okay. "Today I want to be a neurosurgeon." "Today I want to be an astronaut." "Today I want to be a nurse, a banker, a biologist, statistician, chimney sweep, blacksmith ..." Put each of your 30 pieces of paper into a box and at the end of the month, take them out and tally them. What you'll see is an emerging pattern. You'll see that a significant number of your papers in the box have something in common: You have an affinity for doing things with your hands, you lean toward science, you like helping people, you have a penchant for managerial or statistical work. A direction will keep cropping up on those pieces of paper, something that you can start to explore.

MORE WAYS TO KNOW WHAT YOU LIKE

There are a number of ways, in addition to Paper in the Box, to discover your affinity. They're all useful and they're all valid.

GET PROFESSIONAL HELP

You can do as Karen did, and seek the advice of a guidance counselor. Here is how Karen describes what took place for her.

> I'd been in the job market in a variety of capacities for twelve years. My last job, where I met and married Len, was as a buyer for a department store. I retired when I married, and for the past eight years I've played homemaker and hostess par excellence. I've worked very hard at creating a beautiful home. I give perfect dinner parties.

> My husband and I travel extensively and have many friends. But for the past two years, I've been restless. There must be something else more meaningful for me in life. I figured, I'll get back into the job market and get myself a $50,000-a-year position. After all, I worked for twelve years, I've done volunteer work for eight years, and I have a superb contact base. I've got to be paid more than a kid just starting out.

> Well, I didn't know what I was going to do to get that $50,000. So I went to a career counselor for advice. I never saw so many tests. And we had a lot of pretty intense discussions. Finally, we came up with a diagnosis that felt right for me.

> As I said, I'm a good hostess and manager, and I have a strong interest in helping people through volunteer work. Putting those together, we came up with the idea of a career in hospital administration. I used some of those excellent contacts I mentioned and, through them, sat down with a number of administrators to find out exactly what that job entails and whether I would need any additional graduate work to qualify.

Now I have a clear path before me, and I am so grateful to that guidance person. I mean, really, it was crazy of me to think I want somebody to pay me $50,000 right away just because I'm going back to work.

Besides availing yourself of guidance counseling, you can devote several hours a week to writing out lists of career goals and directions or what you would have done if you'd had the opportunity. You can read books and talk to others about career opportunities. Work at it, and a direction is sure to emerge.

TAKE THE MOTIVATION TEST

Here's a third way to help you learn what turns you on so that you can see which direction to take. It's a way to uncover your basic motivation and ascertain what it is you need in life to win satisfaction. Again, it's a written exercise that will help you think things through to specificity. Read through the checklist that follows and write down the word or phrase that you believe is your major drive, the reward you want most. Be very introspective and very honest. Write down the answer on a piece of paper and save it, to refer to later as your needs and self-knowledge strengthen or change.

MOTIVATION CHECKLIST: WHAT'S MOST IMPORTANT TO YOU?

1. Money
2. Approval of others
3. Power
4. Status
5. Social contacts
6. Creativity
7. Challenge
8. Resume and credential building
9. Other drive

It doesn't matter what your answer is; there is no right or wrong, no good or bad. Any of the motivations is valid as long as you are completely honest with yourself. Just know this: The definite desire, the motivation you have written down on a piece of paper, is your strength. There is power in it. It is the fuel for your motor, the force that will drive you to your goal.

IT'S YOUR LIFE; LEAD IT

As women, many of us in the 35-plus age group, are so used to having goals set for us—by parents, professors, spouses, people other than ourselves—that we aim to please them, not ourselves. We work on being conduits for fulfilling their needs and operate according to their standards for us, and we believe that it's wrong to do otherwise. Self-determination is a mind-set we've been taught to feel is wanton; it makes us uneasy. We think that by focusing on filling our own cups of desire we'll deprive another person of our energies, hurt them by our "selfishness." And so, of course, we'll lose them. We'll be ousted because we haven't behaved according to outdated standards. If we decide to grow and develop in a direction that's rewarding strictly for ourselves, goes the belief conditioned by generations of female subservience, we will wind up pariahs.

So what do we need? Something for us or something for them? It's easy to see why we're readily confused. It's hard enough for anybody, man or woman, to concentrate on self-development; it's even harder for most women because we've been so thoroughly catechized to bolster the needs of other people: husband, lover, children, those the world has long held are the Important Ones. They're our omniscient, dominant Wizards of Oz and we feel we're in conflict with them when we don't adopt their goals, identify solely with their needs, act as compliant wife, sacrificing mother, dutiful daughter. But remember what happened to the Wizard when the mythology was stripped away? He became what he'd been all along: real as truth and just like everyone else.

Again, it may seem that I'm stating the obvious, but the truth is this: It's perfectly all right to determine your own future. Today there is no one chart to follow since we've changed so radically. However, you must start someplace and make some determination, knowing that it's going to change. You have the right to start anywhere. *Flexibility* is the biggest goal you can have in life. The affection and relationships you've always had will remain while you grow and develop in your own way. Setting personal goals and standards doesn't mean loss; it's a winning process all the way.

TUNE IN TO YOURSELF

There isn't a career manual or guidance counselor who will not tell you that you have to set goals. But do you *really* pay attention and do it for yourself? Sometimes people don't do it because they're afraid to admit they don't know how.

> I tried so hard to be a good student. I felt so dumb and defeated when I failed my high school equivalency test. I just couldn't study right and become what my mother wanted for me. In order to make a living, I was baby-sitting. My employer kept complimenting my talented hands. I can cook, do hair, and sew very easily. I finally decided to drop my mother's wishes and follow my own. I'm so happy and grateful to be apprenticing as a dress designer now. I'm happy all the time, and my mother seems happy for me, too.

Listen to Angela, who's 28 years old, has already had three successful careers, and intends to have many more.

> People told me I had to have an M.B.A. to get into the high-tech company where I wanted my first job. I took their word for it. I didn't have that credential and I felt so defensive and anxious about it that I screwed up the interview. Now I've learned to find things out for myself by asking questions, not to take what other people say as gospel, or just blindly do what's supposed to be "right."
>
> For a long time I worried about that degree, and when I found a job at another high-tech company, I went to school nights to earn it. Meantime, I got married and my parents said, "You'll have to leave school and your job and move to St. Louis with your husband." I liked my work, I wanted that degree, and I liked Chicago.
>
> It wasn't that I was afraid to go to a new city. I just didn't want to go. I chose to be in Chicago. I talked to my husband and we worked out a weekend arrangement that we both agreed would be fine. And it is.

I've done what I needed to do for myself, he's doing what he needs, we have the time together we both need and my parents and all the other people who said I shouldn't live my life so selfishly, well … it's been the same for me with jobs. My father always told me I shouldn't jump around. I should assess whether or not the job I was taking was perfect, and then I should stay there. That's just not right for me or for the times.

I had really good experiences at the high-tech company where I got my first job, and then I moved on to a biomedical company where there was more opportunity. Right now I'm heading up a university research department. I've decided, no matter what "they" tell me, I'll always be looking for a job if it means more responsibility or more opportunity.

Angela's career points up several success factors that are particularly important to observe if you are in the exploratory phase:

1. She has set goals that will satisfy her, not somebody else, and has "won" each time she reached one.

2. She has realized that it is not necessary to strive only for the perfect, prepackaged life goal or job. That's an impossible fantasy and people who don't see the reality almost always wind up stymied by their own rigidity. They remain dilettantes, touching on this, shying away from that, stifled by fears and mythology.

3. She has built up the knowledge and credentials that have moved her on within her field of interest and that may move her on into others.

4. She has not been afraid to set goals and make commitments to them. She has learned that they are stepping stones and not final destinations.

THE ONLY SURE THING ABOUT THE FUTURE IS THAT NOTHING IS FOR SURE

The thing that makes goals so interesting is that you can always change them. If you're willing to be flexible and open in your thinking—a requisite in every part of the selling process—if you're willing to experiment, to take risks and detours, you will grow and change even as your goals do. Change means growth; in its absence is stagnation.

As a matter of fact, if you think back over your life, you'll see that you are already well attuned to change and its connection with growth. It is intrinsic in every woman's curriculum vitae, the constant in our lives. As a caretaker you have responded to each stage of your child's, your husband's, or any significant other's growth; you had to. What you learned when your child was a toddler or your husband a career neophyte simply did not apply as they progressed. You had to change with them, to meet their altering needs.

Even if your role has not been that of caretaker, you learned to change psychologically as you grew from girl to woman, as male–female relationships around you changed, as the socioeconomic climate shifted. You're an old pro. How well you succeed in applying the concept of mobility to your goals depends on how keenly you hone your innate initiative and creativity, the qualities you've brought from your past.

IT'S ALL RIGHT TO CHANGE DIRECTION

The process of finding direction and setting career goals entails continual change along with your own shifting needs, desires, ideas, and opportunities. It helps to know that goals are sequential, and committing yourself to achieve something within a specific time frame is not an automatic life sentence. It also helps to know that experimenting to find the direction that's right for you is a course that's been followed by the most successful people in the world. Think of Christopher Columbus.

THE EXPERIMENTAL DIRECTION FINDER

Let me illustrate by changing Christopher Columbus into present-day you. Say you decide, as captain of your ship, that you want to sail to Hawaii. You know the direction and you chart your course for the Pacific. En route you come across someplace else that's terrifically attractive. You stop off, are enchanted by what you find, and never do get to Hawaii. That's all right, because you had a direction that got you moving in the first place, and it took you some-place you found you definitely wanted to be. You haven't drifted at all because you started out with direction; the detour you took was a beneficial option.

To expand on the options, Hawaii could have turned out to be where you would spend the rest of your life. Or you could have been going to Hawaii because you love palm trees, but you learned there's more gorgeous foliage in Florida, so you head for where the good palms grow. Or you may have discovered that you really loathe palm trees and can't stand hot weather either, so you choose Alaska as your new destination. What has happened is that you have committed yourself to a specific plan for a short period of time and explored it enough to know if it is or is not for you—or whether some opportunity along the way is more interesting.

Flexibility combined with specific goals has given you the means to cash in on opportunity.

CHART YOUR COURSE

You, the explorer, have found a direction by discovering your affinities. You've defined your basic motivation. You've taken some experimental career trips—either literally or by mentally visualizing yourself very concretely in the role you want to play. Now it's strategy time. How exactly are you going to reach your destination? How will you get from here to there, five years from now? Certainly not in one giant leap. The way to get from here to there is by setting short-term, interim goals: productive objectives you can realistically attain without fear of committing yourself to eternity.

Again, getting your objectives down on paper where you can see them is one of the first and most helpful steps to take. On pages 44–45 you'll find a sample Goal Sheet and a blank one for you to fill in. You'll notice that it is blocked off in three-month, six-month, one-, two-, and five-year columns. Before you start writing things down, study the sample Goal Sheet—it's the one I filled in years ago, when I first decided to develop the Woman's Selling Game Workshop. Let me take you through some of the steps, to help you clarify what you should write down as your short- and long-term goals.

Goals for Woman's Selling Game Workshop

3 Months	6 Months	1 Year	2 Years	5 Years
Explore 6 selling courses	Adapt and create 20 games and role plays	Select 4 assistants and train	Test-market direct mail association with 4 different concerns	Franchise operation
Get brochures	Try our materials through speaking engagements	Teach 2 courses with all materials	Continue collecting testimonials	
Sign up for 2 courses	—department stores	Edit materials	Get publicity	
Read 10 books on sales	—universities	Explore associations		
Visit special business library. Consult librarian for best books.	—women's groups	—Sales Execs Club		
Set aside every Friday for exploratory interviews.	Start mailing list	—National Organization of Women		
See 4 people connected with field each month.	Watch for talent at speaking engagements	—National Association of Female Execs		
Have Judith explore 6 specific pitches, e.g., Tupperware, Shaklee, Avon, Berlitz	Collect 20 testimonials	—American Financial Business Women		
Start file of techniques	Hold 3 discussion sessions with women who have attended speeches, for feedback	Start publicity file		
Start bank account	Invite 15 key women representing groups for idea generation			
	Get lawyer			

Goals

3 Months	6 Months	1 Year	2 Years	5 Years

I started by figuring how much time I'd need for research, what kind of research would be needed, and what the sources were. Certain steps would take three months, another stage would require six months; at the end of a year the research should be completed. I outlined each necessary element in the same way, noting the interim stages and time limits on paper. I listed courses to take, interviews to conduct, outlines to develop, materials to use, and so on.

I'm onto another Goal Sheet by now, of course, but I kept that first one in the top drawer of my desk for years, where I could refer to it constantly, reassessing and making changes every three months in the same way any corporation does. It's been a trusty friend as well as my compass.

Goal Sheets are tools the busiest and most successful people I know use all the time. Steffi, a dynamo who always has at least three different sets of plans going at the same time, underscores something else about writing down specifics. She says:

> Unless I set goals, I won't know whether I've achieved or have gone where I wanted to go. When I'm depressed or angry or discouraged, I'll say, "Oh, I'm not getting anywhere" and bury myself under that. But if I take a look at my schedule, my three-month or five-year plan, I can see that I've done everything I need to do and that this is what's ahead of me. I can see if my career is moving along at the pace it needs to move along, or if I'd better hurry up, or if I had better revise my goal sheet.
>
> Right now I'm on four roads: writing literary criticism, running workshops, getting into counseling, and meeting some people in the book world. So unless I have a clear plan and a structure written down, I'm apt to feel overwhelmed and get very entangled, or feel I'll never get it all done and do nothing. But with structure, all I have to do is tackle the plan piece by piece and it seems to flow along.

GETTING DOWN TO CASES: HOW REALISTIC IS YOUR GOAL?

In order to succeed you have to know what it is you want to succeed in and then you have to get down to cases. The world is a vast toybox brimming with alluring things to sample. And there's an even vaster number of people besides yourself with their hands in the same toybox, grabbing for the same things you want. You need to do some homework before you leap into the fray, so you'll know which end of the box it is feasible to dip into.

One way we help people do this in our workshop is by using the Puss in the Corner exercise with a second rule added. We say, "It's better to be in a corner than in the middle and you may do anything that is necessary to get into a corner." The five players scramble through the exercise five times, and then we ask those who feel they've won, "How did you win?" The answers fly at us. "I won because I noticed everybody else was going clockwise so I went counterclockwise." "I hooked up with a partner and we strategized that if one of us gives up her position, the other could win." "I won because I got a corner four times." "I won when I got a corner once."

At this point we explain again the analogies of reaching game and career goals. First, the people who feel they've won when they've reached a corner, or goal, one or four times out of five now have a set of odds—statistics—that applies to them.

Translating further: If you're looking for a new job in a relatively crowded field—real estate, acting, art, writing, public relations—your statistics may be that you'll win one time for every 30 jobs you go after. In less crowded areas, if you go counter to the traffic or gain the assistance of a partner, you'll enhance your statistics. Viewing the number of wins out of the number of tries as a statistic takes the emotion out of the rejections that are inevitable in any "game" and leaves you with something you can work with on a realistic and productive basis.

I'll give you an example. When I owned a market research company, I could see how the odds changed over a 12-year period: Initially, for every eight proposals we sent out, we could count on winning one job. Then the closure statistic increased to one job for every four proposals. That is, we strategized. As a company with a goal of 40 projects a year, we had to write 160 proposals to win. And when our proposal list got too short, we went to work on an interim goal of lengthening the list, because no matter what, one out of four proposals would come through.

You can set realistic goals by looking at your own statistics. Count up the number of appointments you have made over the last two years, and the number of closures: one out of four, or twenty, or whatever. That's your realistic statistic at this point. Work with it until your odds get better.

BEATING THE STATISTICAL COMPETITION

The people in our exercise who went counter to prevailing traffic won by improving their competitive odds. They could see they were in a crowded field, and therefore selected an area where there was more space. In career terms, the strategy is the same as the one used by a former workshop student, Ellie.

Ellie is in her mid-30s, a brunette with huge dark eyes, very introspective, enormously gifted, and at the same time pragmatic. She has always been very serious about succeeding in her field, which is graphic design. She told me:

> I could see that I was in a heavily overpopulated field. Everybody and his brother and sister is a graphic designer. I thought, "It's madness to vie with a whole world full of designers. The thing to do is carve out a special need that only I and maybe a few others can fill."
>
> I wanted to be different, to have a competitive edge. It happens that I was educated in South America and am fluent in the languages there. I also am keyed into the tastes and mores of both North and South America. So, I figured, that's the special advantage I have over most other designers here. Also, this is an age of specialists and businesspeople like to feel they have a specialist all their own. The thing for me to do is weave my bi-American specialty together with graphic design and sell that to the buyers it would especially benefit.
>
> I studied the marketplace and found that a sizable number of Americans manufacture products for export to Brazil. I went after them! I sold them on my knowledge of South American tastes and my ability to create designs Brazilian consumers would buy. I had practically no competition and I must say, I have the field nearly all to myself.

STUDYING THE MARKETPLACE

It is vital to find out everything you can about the field you're interested in before, as well as while, you're active in it. Thorough advance research will guide you as to whether or not the field is for you in the first place, and provide the information you'll need in order to know how to succeed. Since we're talking about researching your goal, let's say that you think you'd like to go into architecture, or perhaps public relations or direct sales, but you know too little about the field to be sure it's for you.

One excellent way to find out is by talking to a lot of people who are in various aspects of the field. Say it's direct sales. Give yourself a short-term goal of asking ten people who sell something what different types of direct sales exist. Find out what kinds of products or services are sold that way in your area, which of the fields are crowded and which are not. Use business libraries, government agencies, the Chamber of Commerce, directories, every source you can find. Dig in and discover what prerequisites you would need in order to break in: special training, a college degree, a car, a strong body. Don't be reticent about inquiring into every detail that flashes through your mind. Ask somebody if you can follow him or her around for a day, to observe firsthand what it's like to be in that particular field. Inquire on the Internet.

People enjoy helping other people, sharing their knowledge, and presenting informed points of view. Ask enough questions of enough people and you will gain an idea of the options that are available, and which ones are attractive to you. Chances are when you wrote down your major motivation you thought about or wrote down a second motivation as well. It's all right, as long as you were honest about what is most important to you. There's nothing wrong with having a secondary, less urgent drive as long as you know which one is the stronger force, and as long as both are genuine. It's the masked desire that's the troublemaker.

PLANNED PARTNERHOOD

Whether you're role-playing, laboring through the search for your goal, trying to make and hold to tough-sounding commitments, or

need ideas and a pep talk, having a partner is one of the most powerful methods you can use to achieve success. It's like the familiar
buddy system you used when you were learning to swim, when you
and another person were charged with watching out for each
other's welfare. Only the career-building partner system goes far
beyond the swimmer's. Unless you are a constitutional loner—very
highly motivated, experienced, and disciplined—I urge you to
adopt this method.

With a buddy or partner to listen and talk to, you can exchange
information, add to your own experiences, and get feedback, support, analysis, critiques, and advice. You can slice through confu-
sion, digression, and depression. A partner will help you stay on goal
and on schedule. Most of us are simply not sufficiently self-directed to manage all of this solo, or to see ourselves as others see us. We
need the anchor of reporting to another person who will keep our
minds and our efforts channeled in the direction we've chosen.

MAKE A CONTRACT

The partner you select can be a friend or not, and preferably should
come from the same area of expertise as yours so you can understand each other's problems and provide useful mutual assistance.
He or she should be someone whose judgment you respect and
who respects yours, so there will be productive interplay. The two
of you should contract to meet formally and at regular intervals,
once or twice a month, perhaps. Your first meeting may be to define your goals and discuss their reality, with subsequent meetings
devoted to reviewing your progress toward those goals.

When you miss the fact that you've strayed from your purpose,
been vague about strategy, or been laissez-faire about precious
time, it's your partner's job to spot what's happening and give you
the feedback and constructive advice by which you can work
through to what you want. You, of course, will do the same for your
partner in return. As in all good things connected with selling, you
both win.

I've watched the system work well time after time. By creating
a responsibility outside yourself, having somebody to report to and
to be supportive when you're in doubt or fear, you automatically enhance your career power.

Joan and Toby are extraordinary examples of how successful a partnership can be. They'd met at a workshop, when both were ripe to move on to new fields. Joan was a therapist, Toby a marketing consultant. You must be thinking, as they did at first, "But there's nothing in common here. How could they help each other?" Their commonality was that both were competent professionals, both wanted to expand their spheres and, as females, both felt the need for support from a peer. As often happens, the variations in their backgrounds proved complimentary: What need or ability one lacked, the other had. The combination proved both stimulating and creative.

The contract Joan and Toby wrote with one another called for them to meet at lunch every two weeks. Joan recalls:

> When we met, we each had a one- and a five-year plan. We talked for twelve hours, using a tape recorder. When we reviewed what we said, we realized that we could help each other stay on goal if we met and talked regularly. It was obvious we had a great mutual respect for each other's intelligence and ability to get jobs done.
>
> So we wrote out a contract whereby we'd be each other's kick-in-the-pants partner. In it, we agreed to assist one another in every way possible to accomplish our goals, even if it meant phoning each other every day just to nag, "Have you done this, have you met that goal?" We spelled it all out.
>
> Toby's first project in the contract was to make twenty calls within the first two-week period and to accomplish a list of five specific goals. Mine read similarly. At our lunch meetings, we discussed our lists and checked off whether we'd adhered to our time frames. We refined some of our original plans and worked out realistic strategies to implement them. Digressions, ramblings, and vagueness were disallowed per contract, and barrages of questions such as, "Exactly how will you do this; by what date?" kept us both thinking clearly and in specifics.

Joan and Toby got so much done in the first three months, they said, "it was incredible." They wrote out additional contracts, to maintain the enormously productive interchange of help. At the end of six months they found they'd completed all the goals they'd set down in their one-year plans. It was really remarkable. Toby said that "just knowing that on Friday I'd have to sit down with Joan and review my goals and purposes, and compare that with how I used my time, really made me aware of staying on purpose." They gave each other total support; that and their very "oppositeness" gave an energy and freshness to everything they did.

Joan added:

> All this time each of us had been working separately toward organizational work counseling women. One day, we looked at the success we'd had with our partnership and said, "This method works so well, why don't we teach it to other women so they can improve their professional and personal lives as we have?"

> We incorporated ourselves as The Resource Center and the results have been more gratifying than I can say. We provide peer support that develops skills and enhances creativity and, perhaps most importantly, gives women the opportunity to learn from the experiences of others.

The partners-now-entrepreneurs still work on the premise of their original contract, reviewing it formally every three months, eliminating what doesn't work and polishing what does. They are one of the best examples I know of how support from someone who cares about your progress and is willing to give advice can help you advance in your career.

YOU ARE NOT ALONE

The buddy system is worth its weight in restaurant bills if meeting regularly with a partner helps you to make commitments. On your own, without a partner to monitor and assist you, the scariness of putting yourself on the line is apt to put you off—and the result is that you coast and drift, never getting anywhere. That's something that happens to many women, and to men, so don't feel it's shameful. Working together with somebody will help banish your fear.

Once you're committed to the idea of commitment, there's still work to be done. You must not only plot what your future will be five years from now, but also figure out how you'll reach that goal. I can hear your mind clicking: "How do I do that? I don't even know if my company will be in business in five years, much less what my own campaign and strategy should be." You have a point, and if you also have a partner you have a way to get on course.

Make believe. Yes, you keep hearing that fantasy has no place in the selling game, but there are times when visions of sugar plums can be used creatively. It's the purposefully imaginative "What if" springboard that has launched brilliant inventions: "What if a thin wire of tungsten were connected to carbon?"; great novels: "What if three men were to use the Paris sewers to elude the flies?"; and great sales ideas: "What if we hired women to sell kitchenware to other women by arranging parties in their homes?"

More Role-Playing with Your Partner

Just as role-playing helped you uncover a hidden agenda in the last chapter, role-playing with a partner can help you see whether or not you are on track. In this case, the role-playing might more appropriately be called what-iffing, but its purpose is the same—to help you see what is truly possible and to keep you on track.

PAULA PARTNER:	What if this were five years from now and what if you had sold yourself into a position at the top of your dream world? What would you be?
YOU:	I'd be the editor of a national magazine.
PAULA PARTNER:	What kind of magazine? What is its editorial theme? Who are its readers?
YOU:	It's a beautifully illustrated magazine about food, wine, and travel. It's for a very select, sophisticated audience of men and women.
PAULA PARTNER:	Okay. Picture where you are and describe the scene. Who is with you? Why? What are you doing? What is the other person doing? Give me all the details.
YOU:	I'm in my private office at a large white desk. I'm wearing a pale gray suit with a pearl gray silk shirt, and the jacket's off. I've got a great $200 haircut from the guy who does the Vogue covers. The room has a good Turkish carpet and a few shelves of old and interesting tableware—Edwardian pitchers, Georgian tankards, and a half wall arranged with nineteenth-century imported china plates.
	On another ten-foot-long desk are bottles of wine, for a tasting, along with other assorted boxes, opened and

unopened, of food products, tableware, literature about the De Medici cooking school in Tuscany—and piles of stuff arranged on a second narrow table along the other wall. My assistant, a young woman who's a great "computer nerd," is in the office with me, and I'm directing her to update our list of American mini-vineyards and micro-breweries for a special feature story, and to please have the printout for me by Wednesday.

PAULA PARTNER: And you're smiling. Now tell me, what would you have to do in the next six months, starting tomorrow, to attain the nirvana you've just described? Be specific. If I've told you once I've told you a thousand times, wishing and hoping don't count. Is there someone you know who can help you in some way?

YOU: Yes. I'll go see Max Mogul, an editor I now write for. He knows everybody in the magazine publishing field and could give me information as well as introductions to other people who could help.

PAULA PARTNER: That's a good resource and I'm proud of you for knowing right off the bat that you have to build all the contacts you can, to get where you're going. Now, think hard. What else would you need?

YOU: Money. I'd have to start building a backlog of people who've shown an interest in publishing, a special interest in the vast food and "at home" industries, and a willingness to invest in a vehicle, like my magazine, that can promote them.

PAULA PARTNER: How would you prove to your investors that you have what it takes to run a magazine?

YOU: They'd want proof that I have knowledge, experience, and talent, so I'd start adding to my credentials by writing more articles about food, wine, and travel. I'd also get myself on some existing mastheads as a consultant or contributing editor. I also know two hot chefs, one of whom is part-owner in a three-star restaurant, who can write a guest column, and is willing to use some of his most popular dishes, as well as put together lots of others.

PAULA PARTNER: It's a good, clear plan. Have you thought about what you'd have to give up to get what you want?

YOU: There would be certain costs, but I consider them tradeoffs. I couldn't travel with my husband on a few of his international sales trips, as he likes me to do, or take courses for a master's degree in design, a project that's been in the back of my mind for years.

PAULA PARTNER: You have to decide which is most important: being an independent editor of a prestigious magazine, serving your husband's needs, or taking courses in an avocational interest.

YOU: Personal issues are important, but I want that magazine editorship more than anything else and I'm willing to give up what I have to and accept the trade-offs without feeling guilty.

Name anything you'd like to achieve, within the boundary of reality, and play out the five-year "what-if" fantasy for yourself. The only rule is, you must be very specific throughout. And the follow-up is: Follow up!

THE MENTOR METHOD

Hand in hand with the idea of partnering is the concept of mentoring. You've probably had mentors all your life—teachers, relatives, colleagues—people who have done what you're doing before you, who can see your strengths and help you develop them.

A woman I know who now does information processing and analysis for major corporations tells me that she has always been aware of having a number of mentors to whom she could turn at any time. She said:

One mentor who's been very important to me was the person who labeled what I was doing and told me what business I could get into. He was a man I had hired in a previous job to come in and do training. He watched me dealing with people, before and during the meeting, and said, "You have very good training skills."

He began labeling things that he saw me doing as a whole other set of professional skills. I'd thought they were just nice personal skills, hostessing and planning abilities, until he put wholly different labels on them: facilitating, helping people become self-directed. He was right, and I knew it.

He then told me where there was training available in workshops and helped me look in a catalog and pick one out. Then, when I was in graduate school, he hired me to do some co-training work with him. He referred me to two other places, so I helped put myself through graduate school. That's really significant. He literally took me on as an apprentice. My sense is that he in fact saw himself as my mentor. He took great pleasure in teaching me. He has an ego that flowers under the eyes of an apprentice. He likes to be looked up to. As soon as I outgrew the apprentice role, our relationship cooled substantially.

HELP IS EVERYWHERE

Finding a mentor or a partner is not always easy. You may find that you're in a place or phase when the right individuals just aren't available to you. All is not lost. If there's a support group where you live, join it. It's a perfect place to find the help you need, and you can begin to structure your own network. If you're really on your own, you can still create a support system by getting help in one area from one person, adding to it with help in another area from a second person, and so on. The object is to have wise and helpful people assist you in setting and reaching specific goals, so you can have the satisfaction of accomplishment: the knowledge that you have won at what you set out to do.

Many times, there is no *one* mentor for you and you feel disappointment that there is no magic person who will do it for you. The truth is, we've always had mentors, but what we need to do is figure out what piece of each significant person to borrow from. In my personal experience, I've had six or seven different mentors; individually, they haven't been the be-all and end-all, but I've gained important experience from each. I've gained a lot from my partnership with Paul Libin, for example, now vice president of Jujamcyn Theatres, whose business acumen was something I aspired to. He was a great negotiator.

Another person was Dan Yankelovich, CEO of Yankelovich Partners, who taught me the language of research and how to think in terms of finding the research I need. I wasn't specifically following his path, but appropriated the way he analyzed complex situations. I acquired from my mother her creative way of thinking and doing what she did—taking great imaginative leaps to see a way for A-plus-B to equal X. Elly Guggenheimer, a mentor and role model for hundreds of women, founder of the International Woman's Forum and now in her mid 80s, is showing us all how to stay productive and maintain leadership positions in our later years.

Other than individuals, look to support groups like NAFE (the National Association of Female Executives), or women's groups formed from members of virtually every occupation. Every library in America has a copy of *National Organizations of the United States* at its reference desk, a book with an impressive index by subject—there is most likely a group somewhere focusing on your interest, even if you are a suspension bridge builder or the wife of a hog farmer!

Reality: *It's hard to get from here to there alone. Find someone "on goal" to share your journey.*

ORGANIZING FOR SUCCESS

Now that you see why reaching a goal does not happen miraculously, you also have to understand that a lot of organization is involved in getting from point A to point B. You'll need to get yourself organized before you begin the actual work, not after you're halfway submerged in a project. The first step in organizing yourself is to learn to master your time.

YOUR TIME IS YOUR MONEY

Mastering time is the toughest, most dismaying work in the world for some people. But if you're going to be successful, you have to learn to use time, instead of letting it use you. There are only twenty-four hours in each day, and time is a limited, and therefore precious, commodity.

One way to conquer the tyranny of time is to put a dollar value on it. What are you worth—$75, $150 an hour? Then taking time out of your day to type reports or do laundry doesn't make sense. You could hire somebody else to do it at $7 or $15 an hour. That would be a sound, pragmatically realistic investment; by making it you'd retain the full value of your own time.

At $75 or $150 an hour, or however you price yourself, you're going to want to make every hour count. An excellent method of keeping track is to get into the habit of keeping time sheets. Block off each time sheet into segments and write into each segment the time spent, what you did, and for which client or customer. There is great software out there to help you organize your time. At the end of each day or week, when you add up the time devoted to each specific project, you'll see immediately where your profit and loss have been.

THE IMPORTANCE OF PRIORITIES, SHIFTING OR OTHERWISE

There you are with a goal date looming fast and you're nowhere near ready to meet it. Time has somehow gone highballing past and you're frantic. What went wrong? Where did your grip slip? The best way to keep prime targets in sight is to literally keep them in front of you, on your goals sheet.

The best way to keep first things first and prevent less urgent projects from gobbling your time and energies is to make fresh lists of your mini-range projects every day. The very act of writing things down (or making a computer file) forces you to think and plan. The time you spend on advance planning is a gift to yourself: It will shorten the time you spend later on performance.

Schedule each day as it comes. Each priority needs continuous reassessment, as needs and situations change constantly. If there's a store opening up and you're in the business of selling Product X, you can't be dragging your feet and doing final wrap-up details on yesterday's priorities. Drop everything and go to the new store, fast and first.

List each day's appointments in your "power book"—a portable computerized diary/phone book/notebook—or in your computer's datebook program or a handwritten diary: 10:30 conference, 2:00 meeting, 4:00 interview. Make a second list of things to do, in order of their importance or urgency. The top of your To Do list should be things that will take you closer to your goal. If the rest of the list runs too long and can't be completed, review it and eliminate, postpone, or get somebody else to take care of the inconsequential activities, the things you don't really have to do. Otherwise you'll waste irreplaceable time chasing up and down dead-end alleys.

A powerful technique for staying in charge of time is to make yourself accountable to someone else. Very few people are so disciplined that they can keep on goal and stay on schedule without an outside "conscience" as a goad. Use your partner as your goad and write a contract with her that will encourage and force you to adhere to the timetables you've set.

FOCUS ON FIRST THINGS FIRST

Time must be handled on a day-to-day and an ongoing basis, and always with realistic flexibility. If you feel that you can't handle Tuesday's list because you woke up feeling miserable and know you won't perform well that day, defer whatever you can until Wednesday. If your quarterly "corporate review" of your goal sheet shows that changes should be made, make them. Nowhere is it written that there's merit in being rigid.

We're all tempted by things that can tug us off goal. My friend Nancy told me about a near-fatal instance of priority sidetracking that came along while she was studying to be a theatrical attorney and sometime producer. One day, with bar exams a mere six months away, a man named Mr. Showbizz called and said he was backing a Broadway show and would she like to start right away as coproducer. Of course, Nancy's instant reaction was "Is this a miracle? I would love to produce and here's a perfect opportunity dropped right into my lap."

Then she realized that if she waded into coproducing a show, she couldn't finish studying for the bar and would be throwing away her primary goal of becoming a theatrical attorney. Sanity intervened in time and the priorities became indisputably clear. Nancy called Mr. Would-Be Showbizz, explained the situation, and offered to find somebody for him who was immediately available to produce his show. She also put his name in her growing collection of contacts. Later, when her law degree was in her possession and she was ready for the production side of show business, Nancy had that card as a reminder of a man willing to back shows.

Focus on what needs doing now.

THE MAÑANA TRIP

There's another caveat to build into your list-making: a habit. Postponing non-urgent things to do translates, for some people, to falling into the procrastination trap. It's a trip to nowhere, unless you learn to change direction. Here are some constructive habits to substitute for the counterproductive urge to procrastinate.

1. Slice the chore that seems onerous into small, digestible portions and tackle one slice at a time. It will take the "overwhelming" out of the largest task.

2. Whittle down your habit of procrastinating by taking on the tasks you've been putting off, one at a time. Completing one unpleasant chore a day will give you that exhilarating feeling of accomplishment, won't hurt a bit, and will get you into the habit of tackling what needs to be done without sweeping it under the rug.

3. Force yourself to make more lists: two for each job you're procrastinating over. On List A, write the reasons why you're not doing whatever you're not doing, and on List B write down the benefits that will accrue if you get the job done. List A will look silly: "It's boring." "I'm worried about looking good and on top of things—I'll be facing heavy hitters when I ask for that meeting." "I can't think of what to wear." List B will look sensationally attractive: "I'll earn $1,500." "It will be a career booster." And, surely a major reward, "The job will be done and over with."

4. Blend desire with duty. On a rainy morning when you have 30 phone calls to complete and you don't want to get out of bed, satisfy both needs. Be nice to yourself. Bring the phone and coffeepot to the side table near your bed and start calling number one. The people you're phoning will never know where you're calling from, and you will have gotten started despite your stalling, by taking one small step at a time. As someone once said, "If procrastination is your problem, don't put off doing something about it."

RESEARCH: THE MOST IMPORTANT TIME-SAVER

Research is the activity that all successful persons use to avoid wasting their precious hours and efforts on activities that are not feasible. Through research you learn what is and what is not possible before launching into a full-scale attack on a project. Research also makes you more efficient when you do act—and efficiency always saves time. With research properly done, you never have to succumb to the useless fluttering that comes from not being sure where you are going or what your basis for acting is. So many activities—and even goals, for that matter—can and should be avoided because they are inappropriate or won't get you where you want to go. The best way to know what to avoid is to do your research in advance.

Whether you plan to find a job, get a raise, start a new business, or increase your rates, you'll save yourself enormous amounts of time if you dig in and get all the facts before you begin.

ORGANIZING YOUR RESEARCH

As you gather more and more information, and particularly as that information begins to translate into sales, you will want to develop a storage system for your research and sales materials. Keeping data in systemized files is one of the shortcuts to professionalism. In fact, it's essential. Whether you are in business for yourself or are with a company that has its own systems, you'll always need to be able to put your hands on specific information quickly and accurately.

ORGANIZING JOB FILES

One storage system that is a must for the well-organized professional is the job file. Don't wait until you have garnered ten jobs to set it up; start it the minute you get your first job so you'll always be in control. If you're one of the very rare people out there who do not know how to use a personal computer, you'll need to manage your files by hand. But it's smarter to plug into a simple program that can help you produce with greater efficiency.

With so many software programs made for helping you "sort, merge, and retrieve" names, information, statistics—plus the astonishing capabilities of the Internet to connect you to sources all over the world by interest and specialty—you should be able to find a program that suits your needs. Go to a large computer supply store and tell them what you need. They can recommend the best program for your needs, one that will work with the system and printer you've got or intend to buy.

Meanwhile, here are some guidelines for creating a job file; alter them as necessary to fit your personal needs and working method. Such a system is even faster with a PC. So to begin:

1. Assign a number to each prospect, client, or customer you acquire:

    ABC Co. = 1
    DEF, Inc. = 2
    GHI Assoc. = 3

2. Assign a second number to each project for each of the prospects, clients, or customers:

    ABC Co.: 11, 12, 13, etc.
    DEF, Inc.: 21, 22, 23, etc.
    GHI Assoc.: 31, 32, 33, etc.

    After a period of time, those codes could look like this:

    ABC Co.: 1431
    DEF, Inc.: 2210
    GHI Assoc.: 3119

    You can use your master code in a number of ways:

    a. to identify a project's deadline;

    b. to identify a project's work status ("in progress," "canceled," "completed");

    c. to identify a project's estimated and actual cost;

    d. for billing purposes. (You can augment the master code with a file folder system: one file for each project, coded appropriately; "193" for the ABC Co.'s October project, for example, will supply all the time, out-of-pocket expenses, and fee information you need to get your billing out quickly.)

ASSUME YOUR MEMORY IS ROTTEN

Aside from the fact that you should be writing down everything you learn about yourself, your career, and your clients, you will also rely heavily on a filing system to store this information. Files on clients, for example, should contain information on deadlines for projects, the work status of projects, billing information, and estimates and costs. No matter how important the client or the job, do not assume that you will remember important or unimportant information. Assume that you will remember nothing, make and file accurate records, and you will never have to suffer the embarrassment of having to call a client to ask her to repeat information you should have at your fingertips.

Reality: *Successful selling is being well-organized and covering your bases as best you can.*

TOTAL CAREER POWER: GETTING IT AND USING IT

A young woman recently came in to see me for a job. There's no doubt in my mind that she'll go places. She's very bright and talented, and her enthusiasm is great. But she's not willing to be trained right now. She's in too much of a hurry. She won't invest the time and effort required to learn the basics of a job she wants. So she compensates for her lack of knowledge by trying to fake it, which puts her into oversell. I simply couldn't hire her.

As this example shows, one mistake too many women make is thinking that they can make it on enthusiasm alone, or that because they have personal style or professional expertise, they will naturally succeed in selling. They think, "I'm so good at what I do it'll sell itself. What I'm offering is terrific and people will come and seek it out." Or, "I'm so loaded with energy and charm I can talk anybody into anything, even if I don't know very much about what I'm talking about."

Often such feelings are a natural result of the thinking that goes into choosing a goal. You get so enthusiastic over your plans that you forget to assess carefully what you have to sell, what you need to get your career off the ground, and how to move toward the ultimate goal—success.

Expertise and enthusiasm are two qualities you cannot do without. But they are totally interdependent on each other, and on a third vital quality as well: the ability to sell. Professional expertise, positive outlook, and selling ability: the three operating as a totality comprise the dynamic that can make a person truly successful. It is the framework of mature professionalism, the structure whose elements are inextricably linked. Weakness in one diminishes strength in the others; strength in all three underlies every success.

To simplify what total career power is, let's compare it with something with which you are already familiar: the child's board game, Chutes and Ladders. The game, you'll recall, consists of a series of squares, a pair of dice, and markers representing the players. You move around the board according to what turns up on each throw of the dice, sometimes advancing many squares ahead on the ladder and sometimes slipping back down the chutes all the way back to START. The marker that represents you can be in the shape of a perfect pyramid. If each side is as tall and as strong as the others, it will move along wherever you place it. But what if it were lopsided, with one or two of its sides weak? The marker would wobble on the board so that you couldn't move along from space to space and play out the game to win ...

In your career, just as in Chutes and Ladders, you need a balanced pyramid or you'll keep falling off the board.

Let's analyze the pyramid playing-piece that is essential for career power. Within the center of its three sides is you: your persona, your ethics, your style and personality. These are qualities that can be studied in others and nurtured in yourself, but they are personal characteristics and nobody can teach them to you. Nor is there any right or wrong to them per se; what's right is what's comfortable for you. Your style may be subdued or energetic. You may be maternal or commanding. One is no better or more effective than another; style is simply the personal flavor you impart through the manner in which you communicate your thoughts.

Elizabeth has observed a change in her personal style through the years, because she's enhanced her professional, selling, and attitudinal powers. She characterizes herself as informal and straightforward, and feels that in some cases, her style has been "the difference that sells." She says,

> When I first started in business I saw no reason to reveal anything about myself. I'd never open up. You could even see it in my body language: I'd sit stiffly with my knees pressed together and my

arms hugging my chest. Let a client ask something as simple as "Do you have brothers and sisters?" and I'd change the subject—then wonder why it took me so long to learn about them.

I've found, though, that the more business contacts I've made and the more strangers I've talked to, the more open I've become. I show my cards right away now: who I am, what my interests are, things I was so uptight about. I let my personality come through, and it helps us both.

One way I do this is by asking questions. For example, when I go to a client's office on a sales call, I'll look around and pick up a clue to ask something personal about. "Oh, did you take these photographs? Is photography your hobby? It's mine, too." I'll go into it a little bit: "I do my own black and white printing, do you? I picked up a tip recently from a commercial photographer that might interest you." I find that five minutes or so of that sort of opening conversation lets you get something going with a total stranger, and gets them to communicate with you ... even trust you.

Elizabeth's informal entry works well for her: It gets customer and seller both off the anxiety-centered topic of why she's making the sales call. It puts them more at ease and lets her find out a bit more about the other person before she gets down to business. Being direct and honest in manner and giving them something to relate to builds their confidence in her.

Kelly, though, says her caretaking style has evolved from having been the oldest of four children. She told me:

I did a lot of training and explaining things to people who were younger or less experienced than I was. I've transferred that experience to my career now and find it very enjoyable. Growing up as the oldest, I got a kick out of being the expert—the one who'd done it before. I still do.

There's a direct relationship between that childhood feeling and my style in selling to people now. It has carried over into my becoming a person who is like the mentor, the mother, the rock people can rely on.

I think everybody is looking for a parent—a mommy or daddy who will take responsibility and lead them through what they are doing. And I think that's how people view me now.

Your style is as unique as your fingerprints. It's your life experience, your environment, your values. How it enlarges your capacity to succeed depends on the powers you surround it with—your career powers.

THE BASE OF YOUR CAREER-POWER PYRAMID: PROFESSIONAL EXPERTISE

> I've always tried to get things by just selling my eagerness and my willingness to work. And yet, how far have I gotten?

Professional expertise is being very good at what you do, and having the credentials to prove it. The better you are at what you do, the stronger and broader that side of your career-power pyramid is. Whether you're a doctor, a fund-raiser, a hairdresser, or selling someone else's product or service, unless you have expertise in your area, you've nothing to sell.

> **Reality:** *If you don't know what you are doing, you are just faking it. You have to know what you are selling.*

Take Suzanne. She's a travel agent. She possesses enormous selling skills. She's one of those people who can get Inuits to buy snow by the bucket—once. I know, because Suzanne once sold my husband and me on a summer vacation in Vermont that we'll never forget—or repeat. She called us up, effervescing with what she had to offer: "This place is you! It's magnificent, with an incredible beach. I'm looking at a picture of it right now and I can see the most fabulous shells; you could make a collection of them. And there's a gorgeous panorama backing the lake, with trees sweeping across hills that rise straight to the sky. No question, you're going to have the best week of your lives here."

When we arrived, we learned that everything Suzanne said was true; it was what she hadn't researched and didn't tell us that hurt. The place was a mosquito hatchery. The furniture was rickety or peeling with paint. And the lake bottom was so rocky you couldn't swim. It was obvious that Suzanne had never visited the place nor made intelligent inquiries; she'd relied on brochures and let it go at that. She oversold us into that week in Vermont, but she'll never get us—or our friends—as customers again.

Suzanne has enthusiasm coming out of her pores, and gets so excited every time she makes a pitch that her fervor is contagious and people are swept along on the tide of her belief in what she's selling. She's unable to achieve a true career of continuing success so her sales amount to occasional one-shot deals—because she's faking it. She hasn't done more than skim the surface of the travel business, knows only smatterings about destinations and deals, and sells what sounds good at the moment without any substantiation. She lacks professional expertise and until she fills in that gap and strengthens that side of her pyramid, she will always be selling blue sky. Once.

What Suzanne needs to do is take the time to bolster her expertise by attending travel workshops and seminars. She could also join forces with a consortium of experts in her field who could augment her knowledge. She should read up on everything to do with the travel business and get out and experience travel packages for herself. And she can gain the expertise she needs without losing the momentum she has going for her. She can keep right on selling travel and improving her professionalism while she works, if she is willing to sacrifice a few evenings with her friends and family. At this stage, it is essential for her to make a priority of strengthening that side of her career power.

SIDE TWO OF YOUR CAREER-POWER PYRAMID: CONFIDENCE

Confidence, or a positive outlook about yourself and your abilities, is the second important element in Total Career Power. Many women are weak in this area because they've been taught not to present themselves positively or forcefully, and because they have such overwhelming fear of being rejected. Frequently, as in Marjorie's case, the absence of a positive outlook is a complete hindrance.

Marjorie has what Suzanne lacks: professional expertise. Still, she's not successful. Marjorie designs children's clothing. Her ideas are fresh, functional, fun, great-looking, and ought to sell internationally like the latest Barbie doll wardrobe. Yet the samples sit in her studio, collecting dust and going nowhere. Marjorie's problem is twofold. She lacks confidence in *herself*, not her talent; yet she's afraid that if she tries to sell her designs, she'll be turned down. She has admitted:

> I never step out fully, just halfway. I'll sit in my studio and work out something really nice, a design I feel good about. And then I'll let my imagination take over and start seeing myself being rejected. I'll imagine myself going into a buyer's office and being scrutinized, and feeling ... inadequate. I can hear the "No." So my beautiful designs just sit here, because I just never have the guts to take them out and sell them.

What Marjorie could do is go the route of having an agent or rep—someone strongly on her side whose career it is to sell the talents of others—take over the sales end. In that case she'd be a behind-the-scenes person all her life, turning out nice designs, not being in the swing of the marketplace, the sale of her work depending upon the skills of another person.

A great deal of confidence could be learned by hiring a personal business coach. This professional could take her step-by-step through a set of practical exercises and techniques that can pull Marjorie out of her lopsided career-power pyramid. If such one-on-one coaching isn't right for her, she can attend any of a number of support groups, such as assertiveness training workshops, public speaking classes (to gain experience and confidence in talking to a group), or any self-improvement seminar that will strengthen her positive feelings about herself.

She could also read through the very specific books and articles that are so helpful to people who are looking for guidance in learning to project confidence and believe in oneself. Through these efforts she could begin to overcome her fears and self-doubt, and develop an attitude that says, "I can do it and I will do it." With a positive attitude about herself she would be better able to pick up the phone, make appointments with buyers, and get out there and ask for what she wants.

These steps are scary. It takes a lot of practical commitment and self-determination to correct the wobbly playing-piece that is preventing Marjorie from moving from talented dreamer to successful designer.

Reality: *It is not written in stone that making changes is easy.*

Wendy is another talented person whose outlook held her back. She worked very hard and for a long time so that she could move ahead from being fearful and not getting results into giving her playing-piece the power she needed to move up the ladder to WIN.

Wendy was fired from her first job as a publicist for a children's book publisher because, in her own words:

> I was erratic—that is, some of my solutions were good, some were not. My boss couldn't count on consistently good results from me. Later I found out the reason for it. I was afraid—not that the work wouldn't be accepted, but that *I* wouldn't be.
>
> I'd completely confused my goals, if it could be said that I had any. That was part of my problem. I realized what was going on when I got fired—I was out of contact with myself and that frightened me further. I spoke with a friend about it and her advice was to see a therapist. She said, "Wendy, you have a talent, but if your work isn't consistent, find out why. Go get help!"
>
> It was the smartest move I ever made; it made everything clear. Finally, I could acknowledge my own professional talent and believe, "I'm good. It's what I can and will sell. It's what I can learn how to market properly, now that I'm aware it's not me people might reject, but my work as a publicist."
>
> Gaining that awareness of myself was a long, slow process, but now I know how to use what I have. Now I can follow through on my goals, improve my work skills, and know I can succeed.

Almost everybody experiences self-doubt and is scared at some time. Helen, who once had a problem with shyness, developed the confidence and expertise that allowed her to move forward. She capsulizes the attitudinal aspect of her 14-year career this way:

> Before I began selling, I doubted that I could do it or that I would enjoy it. Once I started, my attitude changed radically. Selling was very different from what I expected. I thought that I'd have to push harder than I did, and that I'd be very uncomfortable dealing with people. The two were interconnected in my mind, and I was sure I wouldn't be any good at all.

But getting out there and doing it has taken Helen way past that defeatist attitude. And getting beyond those feelings not only has made selling easier, it has made it pleasurable for her. She's gone from shyness to enjoying the opportunity of meeting interesting people. She continued:

> You know how sometimes you find somebody you just enjoy talking to, and even when you don't, you sort of file that person away as an interesting character? I can do that now, freely. The one thing I've learned is that positive feelings and confidence in yourself keep building.
>
> When you take a chance and get the thing that you want, reach the goal you've set, you get strength from that. You look at it and say, "I got that. If I can do that, I can do this." And then you go on to the next goal and say, "I got A and B and now I can get C. I'm just going to go for it." You keep building and building.
>
> People can give you the traditional arguments about why you shouldn't do what you want to do, and why you'll never succeed to the top because you're a woman, but you're the only one who can prove to yourself whether you can or cannot get what you want.

Helen proves that *making the effort* is important. Even if it doesn't turn out the exact way you want it to, *you did it.* You set that goal and you worked at it with the idea that you could win. One-third of selling is having the confidence that you are going to succeed at whatever you try. Confidence gives power to your career playing-piece.

SIDE THREE OF YOUR CAREER-POWER PYRAMID: SELLING ABILITY

Now we come to Joanna. She is one of the best journalists you'll ever meet: a thorough researcher, a deft writer, conscientious about deadlines. As a free-lance reporter she's near-Pulitzer-Prize caliber, and she knows it. Her attitude about herself and what she does is thoroughly upbeat.

So there are two solid sides to her pyramid playing-piece: She has professional expertise and she is confident and optimistic. But Joanna has been looking for a job for nearly a year and at this point is blocked from ever getting anywhere because of the one skill she is missing: the ability to sell herself. The woman has no idea how to go about persuading people to want what she can give them.

The editor-in-chief of a suburban newspaper told me how Joanna's been operating. Right now, being editor of the paper's Living Section pages is a job she wants so much she can taste it. It's a job she'll never get, despite her competence. What she did was walk into the editor's office and tell him how she was going to take over the show. Just like that. "Look," she as much as said, "you have a problem and you're incapable of handling it, so you'd better turn it over to me."

Joanna approached the editor as if he were an idiot who didn't know what he was doing, leaving neither of them with a way to win. Making her prospective employer look bad was fatal to Joanna's ambitions, because making somebody wrong is the cardinal sin in selling. She could have won him over, instead, by showing him how she could fit into his needs and existing organizational structure.

The editor's response, to himself, was, "I need a team player here and this one's a takeover artist. I want someone who'll support what we're doing, an editor I can rely on to follow my concepts and structure, not a boxer. She may be a champion editor and writer, but I don't want to do combat with a fighter who I know will try to get me to sweat and shove me into corners every step of the way. I wouldn't have her on my staff no matter how good she is."

Reality: *Selling is strategy—not takeover.*

Creating a win–win situation is one of the selling skills many women, like Joanna, need to learn. Success goes hand in hand with working cooperatively and constructively with other people's ideas, and with assessing situations ahead of time or at least on the spot, instead of making assumptions. Remember: You are always at the heart of your career playing-piece.

In terms of selling ability and style, Pam is the flip side of Joanna. She knows very well the pitfalls of making another person wrong—any person, not just someone she's selling to at the moment. She tells a story of having been invited to a dinner party given by the large realty firm she works for. At the time, she was in a stepping-stone phase of her career and was intent on getting a promotion as soon as possible. She says:

> There were a lot of executives at the party, people I wouldn't normally have had a chance to talk with. One of them asked me questions about what I thought the company's weak spots were, how we could increase our sales. There were several things at the time that I thought were not right. For example, at the lower management level there wasn't enough structure behind the salespeople to let them function effectively.
>
> I was in a funny position since I was working in the department we were talking about—and what I said could place the blame on the sales manager's shoulders. I had to be very careful. I didn't want to make anyone else look bad. I had to keep the dialogue sort of philosophical, not get personal or point the finger, because that's not what it was about. It was about business, in general.
>
> I had to think very carefully before I spoke, because even though I wanted to get ahead, I didn't want my heel marks on somebody else's back. That kind of climbing tactic always boomerangs.
>
> This incident was a big learning experience for me. I realized the ramifications of what could possibly happen if you tip a conversation a certain way. You have to think ahead all the time when you're chatting—and be alert to when someone else is fishing for dirt and hoping to trip you up—or when you're making a hard pitch. You have to be direct and honest but you have to be careful not to create losers. If you do, you'll be a loser, too, in the end.

ASSESS YOUR CAREER POWER

How strong or how lopsided is your career-power pyramid? To get a picture of where you stand and what area needs the most work, make an honest evaluation of your three sides as they are at this very moment. Rate yourself on a scale of 1 to 10 as follows: 1–3: Needs improvement; 4–6: Fair to good; 7–10: Very good to excellent.

Take the opportunity to come back to your game piece when you have completed the book to see how your score has changed.

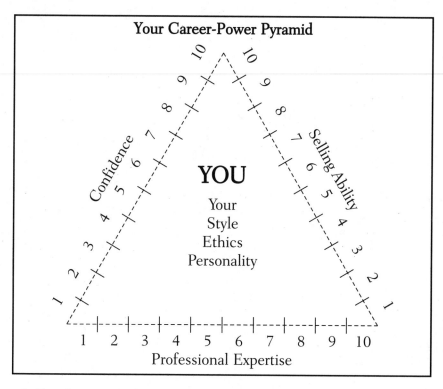

I. To evaluate your professional expertise:
   1. Rate your credentials or educational degrees. _____
   2. Rate your work experience in your field. _____
   3. Rate your life experience touching on your field. _____
   4. Rate how well you know your product. _____
   Total _____
   Divide by 4 _____

II. To evaluate your confidence:
   1. Rate how confident you feel about your professional expertise. _____
   2. Rate how confident you feel about selling. _____
   3. Rate how clear and confident you are about your immediate goals. _____
   4. Rate how clear and confident you are about your long-range goals. _____
   Total _____
   Divide by 4 _____

III. To evaluate your selling ability:
   1. Rate how well your product stacks up against the competition's. _____
   2. Rate your ability to get leads. _____
   3. Rate your ability to make appointments. _____
   4. Rate your ability to tell your product story convincingly. _____
   5. Rate your ability to close a deal. _____
   Total _____
   Divide by 5 _____

THREE LITTLE WORDS: THE BIG THREE IN SELLING

I can't stand rejection. I guess that's what keeps me from making the calls I know I should be making. I mean, there's a good chance the person will say *No* to me if I call. I think people should call me when they want something. They ought to know I do good work, and it's for sale.

You are going to hear one of three answers every time you sell, whether you are selling yourself, a product, or a service. The answers you'll hear will be *Yes, No,* or *Maybe,* and you'd better learn all you can about each, because *Yes, No,* and *Maybe* will be the base you'll work from in selling. This chapter explains how to cope with each of the three answers.

LET'S HEAR IT FOR "YES"

If I asked you, "Which of the three words do you want to hear most?" you'll probably say what everybody says: *Yes.* You'll be absolutely right, of course. For anyone in selling, *Yes* is the best word ever invented. It's what you've been working to get: the agreement from someone to act on or buy what you have to offer. No question: A *Yes* is paradise gained—for most.

There are some people who have difficulty when they hear the word *Yes.* Tell them, "Yes, the job is yours," and they immediately start unselling themselves:

- "With longer hours, how much more of my money will go to pay the baby-sitter?"
- "Now that I've got a bigger job and I'll be earning more than my fiancee, he's going to feel threatened. I know he'll leave me."
- "How will I coordinate a vacation with my husband?"
- "I can't leave my old job before I finish reorganizing the computer system—I couldn't possibly start for another two months."

The problem is, they're so sure nobody could really want them, they're foreseeing only failure. The *Yes* takes them by surprise and they've no idea how to deal with it. The trouble with a lot of people who can't take *Yes* for an answer is that they have a hidden agenda not to succeed and their whole attitude is built around *No*. Gina's story is typical.

Since we've been living in the West Indies, I've been painting in a realist style, and for the past two years my theme has been tropical flowers. I did a series of twenty-four paintings, each one related to the other, and I loved having them around my studio. Recently my husband had to go to Florida on business, and I went along and set up appointments with Miami art dealers and gallery owners. I lucked out on the first try.

A patron of mine had introduced me to a dealer whose tastes were similar to hers. In forty minutes the dealer had purchased three of my paintings and taken eight on consignment. She offered me $500 for each, and I grabbed at it. I was elated ... until I walked out the door.

Suddenly I felt depressed and upset. I had accepted her offer to purchase too quickly. I didn't know if $500 was a fair price, and worse, I was giving up my babies. The series was no longer complete; I didn't know if I'd done the right thing and I was pretty miserable.

I stayed up all night and called the dealer first thing the next day, saying I wanted my paintings back. She became very agitated over my unprofessionalism, so I didn't make a definite appointment to go pick them up. I began calling my painter friends to ask what to do, though it was a little after the fact.

I finally understood that the $500 was a fair price and, as one friend told me, what was wrong was that I was going through the feeling of having given birth and then watching the child leave home for the first time. I'll probably always have that feeling, but I can't hang on to everything I produce. They have to go out into the world.

WHAT'S THE WORST WORD YOU CAN HEAR?

You'll probably give the same answer most other people give, too, if I ask you, "What's the worst word of the three?": *No.* You'd prefer to hear *Maybe* because it seems to imply there's still hope. That's like the captain of the Titanic facing the oncoming iceberg and taking action by saying, "Maybe if we quickly rearrange all the deck furniture so it tips the ship the other way... ." It's a fantasy.

The reality is, *Maybe* is the worst word you can hear.

I'll explain more about the perils of *Maybe* in a minute. First let's explore the value of a good, resounding *No.* It is valuable. Not as good as a *Yes,* but light-years better than *Maybe.*

NO IS A WORD YOU CAN WORK WITH

I was always somebody who felt more comfortable hearing *Maybe* than *No,* because then I could hold on to my fantasy about what might happen, and because it meant I didn't actually have to confront a *No.*

Imagine yourself in this scene: You've gone into an interview with your goal clearly in mind and the facts concerning your product or service properly marshaled. You've spoken persuasively in terms of what you can do for the company and not what the company can do for you. You've given the interviewer your best, and his or her answer is—a dagger through the heart: *No.*

The reality is, *No* is not a dagger; it's a wonderful opportunity, one to take advantage of quickly. Rather than going berserk, losing your focus, and forgetting why you're there (do you know the feeling?), you react to the answer in a straight, collected manner. You are immune to the word *No* as a negative, and hear it instead as a door-opener to questions you'll ask that can change *No* to *Yes.* Notice, I said questions, not statements. You're inquiring, not attacking; respecting your interviewer's opinions; never making him or her wrong. Here is how you can use *No* to elicit information that can help you make the sale.

INTERVIEWER: No, I don't see you for this particular job.

YOU: I see. Let me ask you a question. What qualifications would I need in order to come back and see you again in six months?

OR

INTERVIEWER: No, what you propose is out of the question at this time.

YOU: You say "at this time." Apparently you feel there will be a time when we can talk about my proposal. Perhaps there's something else right now, an obstacle you haven't mentioned. Are delivery schedules a problem for you?

Your questions might reveal that you got a *No* simply because the other person didn't understand everything about what you were trying to sell.

INTERVIEWER: No. Your fabrics don't fit into my color scheme.

YOU: I notice that you like sunny colors. As a matter of fact, these fabrics not only come in the blues I showed you, but also in yellow. And I can get any of the other shades that tie in with yellow for you. Are you planning to do the whole house in those tones, or just this room?

The *No* you heard was not a loss. It was a wedge. It gave you a way to find out why he or she said *No*, and to get suggestions for alternate routes to your goal, other needs you might fill. It let you find out when or how it would be feasible to try the sale again. It let you make discoveries.

CHANGING *NO* TO *YES*

It doesn't bother me any more when somebody says *No*. I can just go and get *Yes* somewhere else later on. And the *No* doesn't hurt because I know it's for the product I'm selling, not me personally.

Linda, a fashion coordinator, thought of a way to extend her expertise in grooming women to benefit large corporations by providing complete styling, from clothing and accessories to makeup and hairstyles, as services for their employees. The employees would benefit from her help and so would the corporations, in terms of having better-groomed, more poised employees. She made an appointment and presented her fashion package service to an airline company for their attendants and reservations clerks. The immediate response was negative: "But you've never done a whole program for anybody before."

Since it was her first attempt at providing total fashion coordination for a corporation, Linda was momentarily tempted to dodge the issue and fake her experience. Wisely, however, she faced the challenge honestly and said:

> You're right. I haven't done this whole program for anybody else before, but I am confident the pieces fit. What I'm proposing is custom-tailored to your organization. It is based on my expertise in knowing what to do and how to do it. I'm certain that you'll be pleased with the results in terms of employee morale and the image you present to your public.
>
> Let me tell you a way we can try it out without your having to make a large commitment right away.

What Linda did in this case history was change a *No* to a *Yes* by being forthright and positive, and by making it easy for her prospect to act.

A *NO* IS NOT A LOSS, AND IT ISN'T FOREVER

A *No* is not the end of the line; it is fertile soil you can seed so a *Yes* will blossom. Nor is *No* a battleground. When it's the correct answer, based on reality, you can accept it pleasantly, put it behind you, and go on to sell to the next person. A reality-based *No* has one highly desirable quality: It completes a cycle for you and lets you get on with your work. It's a definite answer, a conclusion to the project you are working on.

A *No* is nothing to get emotional about. It is not someone disliking you personally; it's just another statistic. Every selling job has statistics. You may need five contacts to connect on one interview, or your statistics may be that one of every four persons to whom you pitch your product will buy. So think of each *No* as another statistic: If you know you need to collect five *No's* to get a *Yes*, then one more *No* merely puts you statistically closer to your goal.

A *No* is not fatal. It may represent temporary loss, but remember this: Nobody wins them all and nobody loses them all, either.

There's one more thing a *No* is not. It is not your anxious mother or autocratic father barking, "No, don't touch this! No, don't do that!" You're not six years old now and you won't be sent to your room, so your mature response to *No* is to recognize your conditioned reflex as an old acquaintance perched on your shoulder. Acknowledge it. Tell it, "Hello, we've met before and I know what you're all about. For a moment you made me feel I was sinking, but now I'll just get on with what I know I can do."

MAYBE IS THE WORST WORD IN THE BOOK

You may think *Maybe* is a lifeline, that as long as somebody hasn't said *No,* you have a chance. Not so. *Maybe* is a mire that can bog you down and lead nowhere. It's perilous territory to be ensnared in, and you'd best get out as quickly as possible.

A *Maybe* really is to put you off or get rid of you. Unless you reshape it to a definite *Yes* or *No,* it is a worthless answer you can't do a thing with. "Maybe we'll hire more people in February." "Maybe we could talk about it sometime when you're in town again." "Maybe ... I don't know." A *Maybe* leaves you in limbo, stranded, unable to move. You've no objections to answer, no points to parry. The best thing, the only thing to do with *Maybe* is refuse to live with it any longer than you have to.

Reality: Maybe *isn't opportunity knocking; it's a bad rap.*

TWO KINDS OF *MAYBE'S*

There are two kinds of *Maybe's*. One is the real postponed decision, when the person you're selling to has a valid reason for delay. The real *Maybe* is fatal only if you let it hover too long or indefinitely. Therefore, the way to deal with a long-playing *Maybe* is to shorten its duration: Give it a specific due date.

For example, you could nudge it along with a response like, "You say, 'Maybe we can work something out in a few months.' Good. That gives us both time to think through my proposal. Do you agree that a month and a half would be a reasonable length of time in which to arrive at a decision? Then let's make an appointment to meet then and resolve the situation." The *Maybe* is still there, but it's no longer a treacherous mire because it's been assigned a feasible deadline.

You can even strengthen your chances of changing *Maybe* to *Yes* in a case like this. "You were saying that John likes to be involved in these situations. Do you think it would be a good idea for me to talk to John before I come back in a month and a half? Then the three of us can sit down and come to a decision." Now you've not only shortened the *Maybe* time span, you've added an element to it that makes it more likely you'll be moving toward a *Yes*.

> Just clarifying whether an answer really means *Yes, No,* or *Maybe* has helped me save an enormous amount of time. It also saves a lot of anxiety because I think there's nothing that produces more anxiety, at least in my business of fund-raising, than hearing a *Maybe*.

The other *Maybe* is the one you get from someone, who, like all of us, hates to say *No* and for whom *Maybe* is the easy way out. The thinking is, "Maybe if I say *Maybe* rather than *No*, this person won't dislike me." (Even equivocators like to be liked.)

Maybe is also the answer you get from the quavering buyer who's afraid to make decisions. The placating or indecisive *Maybe*-maker needs your help, so you can both climb out of eternal limbo and reach a conclusion.

When he or she mutters something vague such as, "Maybe, I'll think about it"—leaving you not knowing if you'd make the sale or should go and look elsewhere—your most useful response is an inquiry along the lines of, "What other options are you considering? Do you have someone else in mind to fill your need?" Or, "Obviously, you're interested in what I can do for you or you wouldn't be considering what I've said at all. Perhaps I can help you in making the decision. Tell me, will our size range work well for you? Do your stores need more junior sizes than you've been displaying?" The answer will give you the information you need to eventually reshape the inconclusive *Maybe* to a final *Yes* or *No,* and free you to go on from there.

HELP FOR THE UNDECIDED

Many people really have a hard time making decisions. It's your job to help them. One technique you can use is to write down the pros and cons of the situation as you talk, so the other person can visualize the advantages and disadvantages. Build up the list of all the advantages first, writing them down one by one as you stress the positive, and then address the negatives.

For example, suppose you're a sales representative for a dress company. The buyer, your prospect, is having trouble making a concrete decision. You say, "I can hear that you're having trouble making up your mind. Let's evaluate the line in terms of your needs. We'll check off each factor. From what you've said, you find the line innovative, is that right?"

Of course it's right; what you're doing is beginning to get the agreement you'll try for all the way through your meeting. "The styling is fresh; let's put that on our list. It's young; do you agree with that? And it's the right price. Good! There seems to be something still holding you back, though. Is it the size range? I know you specialize in small sizes and petites and it's true this line doesn't come in petites; is that the problem? No? Then we'll write 'size range' in the Advantage column. You say you had some trouble last year with my company's deliveries? We promised you a shipment in three weeks and you think you wound up last on the list. I see; deliveries are a crucial problem."

Now you've succeeded in exposing the problem and can go ahead and figure out how to do something about it, without making idle promises. "I'm going to have a session with Stan, who's in charge of traffic at our plant, to see about establishing priority shipments for you. Are we in agreement that if I call you back this afternoon and guarantee that your orders will receive priority attention, you'll be willing to participate in the fall line? Good! I'll have the contract on your desk by five o'clock."

ACTIVATING A FIRM ANSWER

Another technique for moving the prospect who's interested in what you are selling but can't make a decision is to move her into an answer—by giving her a reason to act. It's the scare technique, really, using phrases like "This may be too premature for your company" that imply you'll go to the competition with your innovative concept and he or she will miss the boat.

Then try to close the sale, or at least move closer to clarifying each of your positions.

YOU: I want to be fair with you about this because you look as if you are interested in what I'm describing. Is that true?

PROSPECT: Well, yes. I just don't know if what you propose is right for us at this time. I'd have to talk with some other people around here.

YOU: That's fair. Why don't you talk to them and meanwhile I'll set it up so you can have an exclusive on our product. Would you say three days would give you enough time to talk to your people?

PROSPECT: Actually, no. This is a huge organization and I have to clear it with a lot of people.

YOU: All right. What would be the time frame you would need?

PROSPECT: I could get the answer in two weeks.

YOU: Fine. I'll phone you then, in two weeks, to get your answer. If it's *No,* that's all right too. I'll try you again.

Sometimes you're faced with an undecided prospect and a bureaucracy to plough through, too. It's not difficult to deal with if you understand how to shape your prospect's behavior. Watch this episode:

YOU: I can see that you're interested in having your junior executives attend our management training conference in October, and what's holding up your decision is all the department heads who have to okay the project. I'm just afraid that there are going to be a lot of other companies who'll want their people to attend the same conference, and you'll lose out. What I'll do is pencil in the reservations for you now, and if anybody else asks for those dates I'll call and let you know about it.

You've done two things here. You've motivated your prospect into walking the project through the bureaucracy for you. And you've presented the conference in such a way that the client can see it as something real that is going to happen.

Now you can go on and extend the reality of your presentation to activate the decision making: "If we set this conference up for you, how many people will attend? Our audiovisual room seats thirty people, and I can reserve all thirty spaces for you if you wish, or as many as you'll need. There's a special training film that suits your industry particularly well. I'll see if I can order it right away because I'm sure it'll mean a successful conference for you."

Now your prospect has solid ammunition and will press for the okays needed to give you the order. His or her *Maybe* will soon become a firm *Yes* or *No*.

THE WELL-ROUNDED *YES, NO,* OR *MAYBE:* COMPLETING THE CYCLE

The reason *Maybe* is so tough is its nowhereness. It leaves you dangling, unable to complete the cycle you've begun. It's the endless song, the joke with no punchline. The incomplete cycle can drive you to lunacy. I know that what completely shatters me is when I'm talking to my husband and he doesn't respond. I can't focus on anything else that's going on until I'm acknowledged, assured that I've been heard and understood. You've had experiences of your own.

Perhaps you've arranged to meet a friend at a restaurant so that you can talk over a certain problem. You sit down, give the waitress your orders, and she doesn't write, nod, or repeat what you've said. The cycle is not complete, and you and your friend can't get the conversation off the ground. You're dwelling only on whether your soups and salads are on the way.

That's what a *Maybe* does to you. *Yes* or *No* supplies completion; a *Maybe* is the undropped shoe. If you think about it for a moment, you can see how the completion of cycles comes up over and over in selling, just as it does in life, and how important it is to write *finished* on a project. When you sell a product or service, get a job or a raise, reach somebody by phone or get the appointment you've been shooting for, you've completed a cycle. Left incomplete, it's like a game that's unfinished: There can be no winner, ever.

HOW TO MEET THE PEOPLE YOU WANT TO SEE

THE RULE OF THREE

I haven't a clue in the world as to how to get started in a career. I mean, I don't know a soul in the business world I could offer my services to. Sure, I entertain a lot and have a lot of business-people in my home. But so what? I was taught that it isn't nice to ask guests for anything for yourself. Anyway, why should they want to help me?

You have a product or service to sell, and you don't know the right people to sell it to. You would prefer not to call on anybody cold, and you figure that because Mr. or Ms. Prospective Buyer is not sitting on the end of your nose, you'll never get to meet him or her. But think for a moment. How do you suppose other salespeople get their contacts? Very simply, they use the contacts they already have to develop new ones.

Let me ask you a question:

CAROLE: Who would you like to meet next week?

YOU: Brad Pitt.

CAROLE: Okay. I don't know him, but I know somebody who's a friend of his agent. I'll speak to my contact and have him put you in touch with Brad Pitt's agent. The agent will put you in touch with Pitt directly if you have something that's going to benefit his client.

What was just demonstrated is that you can get to anybody you want to, by the *Rule of Three*. One person always leads to another, who leads to a third. It's a human chain. By the Rule of Three, every person you know in the human chain is worth thirteen people. Here's how it works. The first person you talk to can steer you to three good contacts. Each of those three will lead to three more contacts of his or her own. Add it up: Three people times three contacts each, plus your original contact, with his or her three, equals thirteen valuable people.

THE IMPORTANCE OF THE RULE OF THREE

The importance of contacts and the Rule of Three cannot be overestimated. It's a rule successful people use *every day of their selling lives*. As a matter of fact, it's something you've been using all your non-selling life, too. Remember how you found your dressmaker? You asked a friend who she used for alterations, and she gave you her dressmaker's name and phone number. Or else she asked a friend of hers for the name of a good dressmaker. You got to the person you wanted by using a contact, and you didn't feel you were being rude or aggressive by asking. It's no different in selling. One person leads to another, and nearly everybody enjoys the feeling of helping someone else.

ADVERTISING FOR LEADS

In selling, you'll use contacts constantly. Say your goal is to work with a group of paleontologists doing DNA research on dinosaur bones, or to get a job as a dental hygienist in a large periodontal practice. The best way to advertise your need is to talk about it. Get the word out. Discuss your goal with everybody you meet who could conceivably lead you to a paleontologist or a dentist—the person who needs someone on staff with your skills. The more you put out the word, the more chances there are that somebody instrumental will recall your goal at a key moment and help you move readily toward it.

CONTACTS AS CALLING CARDS

Contacts also provide the identification and credentials that open doors to people who never heard of you. Successful people use them all the time. When you have to make a cold call, the first thing to do is name-drop, making a connection through a mutual contact. Telephone and say something like, "I was talking with Jack Fastfood the other day and he suggested I call you to make an appointment. He thought you'd be interested in a project my company's been working on."

Introducing yourself by attaching a name to what you're asking for invariably takes the "cold" out of cold calls. It's an unwritten rule of business life that no matter how harried an executive is, if somebody calls and a friend or colleague's name is attached, you give that person extra attention.

KEEP TRACK OF YOUR CONTACTS

Good contacts have tonnage, and as a good salesperson you should collect them for when you need weight to throw around. A very efficient method is to open a file in your computer software and name it *contacts* or *connections*. Record every potential contact's name listed alphabetically. If you're still working with paper, keep a box file with 3 x 5 index cards and follow the same procedure.

Computer files (or cards) should also contain the crucial information that can be lost from memory: name, address, phone number, business affiliation, where and when you met, the circumstances and conversation, specific people and things that were mentioned.

> **Reality:** *You can meet anybody in this world you need to meet by using the Rule of Three.*

THE PEOPLE YOU'LL SEE ON APPOINTMENTS

In order to make an appointment to sell, you have to have somebody to sell to. Therein may lie a catch: The somebodys who are your sellees may not always be the people you'd choose as friends. The reality is that irrational beliefs and prejudices about who you ought to mingle with or sell to can get in the way of your reaching your goal.

Again and again, I meet perfectly capable women who live on leftovers from childhood, still taking on faith what their elders taught: "Nice girls mix only with nice people of our own kind." Move on! I tell these women it's time to lose your little-girl emotional baggage. Trade it in for logical reality: The reason you sell to someone is because selling is your goal, not because the person is cultured, genteel, or of your religion or race.

My friend Barbara told me a story that illuminates the issue of who you're willing to sell to. She was giving her son a birthday party and asked who he'd like to invite. David reeled off a list of friends, but omitted Louie, the boy with whom he played baseball every day. Puzzled, Barbara asked why. David explained that the reason he played with Louie every day was because he was *a good pitcher,* not someone he'd like to pal around with on any other occasion or invite to his party.

At age ten, David already understood that it is not only all right, but also desirable to deal with somebody professionally with whom you'd have nothing to do personally. Being "nice"—whatever your definition of nice may be—has nothing to do with having a good pitching arm.

Then there was the man who came to address one of my workshops and inadvertently taught us a lesson on who you're willing to sell to. "Bob" was a very shrewd negotiator and master of seizing the opportunity, but so was he an archetypical male chauvinist—opinionated and arrogant. He called us "you girls" and made weak jokes about women's monthly mood changes being responsible for some of our career lags. We'd all heard it thousands of times before—and wondered where he'd been socially and politically the last 20 years.

After the class one student cornered me, irate and sputtering. She wished I'd never asked Bob to speak, he'd spoiled everything for her, and she would never, ever sell to a person like that. We sat down and I asked her the eye-opener question: "Then who *would* you sell to?" I asked her if she thought all her customers had to look like her, have her values and her style, dress like her, use her language. When I told her *my* customer criterion—I sell only to people who pay their bills—she got the point.

PEOPLE WORTH SELLING TO

There's a way of spotting who is and who isn't worth selling to. When you find a person or company whose attitude is to survive, forget them. You're not going to get paid, in cash or anything else, because a survivor is one who's hanging on by the fingernails, grasping at whatever or whoever might keep him or her minimally alive. Survivors are at the bottom of the sell-to ladder.

Perched one rung above is the company or person whose dominant theme is security. They watch their money and their positions very carefully, and need all kinds of proof that you are the right person or have the right product or service. They need to get their security from other people. You can do business with them, but with caution. They'll try to whittle you down: "I can't quite afford that, but if you'll do it for two thousand dollars less ..." Either get yourself a tightly written contract or forget the security-ridden prospect. You need a guarantee, with that type, that you're not wasting your time and talent.

At the top of the ladder is the best type of all, the "social" company or individual. They're characterized by being open, willing to spread out. They're generous, share creative thoughts, develop ideas along with you, and are joyous when you both benefit. "Social" is a winner: a proven, actualized, self-confident, and cooperative person or company who's fun and rewarding to work with.

THE CHARACTERS YOU'LL MEET

There are myriad types of people you'll meet as sellees. Some of them wear faux denim and white socks with black shoes, but underneath the outfit may be somebody who's worth your selling time. Or perhaps not; you have to assess the value of the time the person will require and make your decision accordingly.

THE WHIRLWIND

This is the very busy person who never has time, whose thoughts are never in sequence, whose actions have nothing to do with the discussion. The real problem is that Whirlwinds are so disorganized they can't keep appointments, make commitments, or be logical. They'll consume your time as if it were tap water. But if they're a real opportunity, the only persons who can make the deal, you'll just have to put up with Whirlwinds. An acquaintance who's a TV news director is in that position. He really has only limited outlets where he can sell himself. So he has no choice but to stick with those outlets, even though it's torture to pin down the people he must meet with.

THE PLACATER

This is the nicest person you ever want to meet—for now, let's make her a woman. She says everything she thinks you want to hear, short of a definite *Yes* or *No*. She's too scared of rocking the boat to make any decisions. Your job is to move her out of *Maybe*. An effective way to do that is to make her your passport to the person who does have the power to buy. Take the Placater along with you as you move up to where the power is. Enlist her aid and make her look good in the process.

Let's assume you're selling travel packages for executives and the Placater has been ever so nice, but won't make a commitment to buy. "We'll see. It sounds lovely, but we'll see." Now's the time to suggest a three-way meeting with Jane Buyingpower, where you can back up the Placater in presenting the package you want to sell and wind up with a three-way win.

THE COMPETITOR

This one's no fun. Has to win, no matter what. Always has to be right, tops you all over the place. If you cite an example of a successful travel package you've put together for another company, he'll tell you about the one *he* invented that's even better. You say the cost of a group charter to Las Vegas is $800 per person; he knows for a fact it costs $810. You can't beat the Competitor at his own game and it doesn't pay to try. The prime rule of selling is never, ever to make anybody wrong; with the Competitor, if *you're* right that means *he's* wrong. So help him be right, since that's what he so desperately needs. It's what you'd do anyway if you were selling to somebody who didn't have to keep displaying how terrific he is. Whether it's worth your time and irritation depends on the Competitor's value to you as a purchaser.

The Blamer

Whatever you say, you're going to be blamed for something. Things are always somebody else's fault, with the Blamer. "Toni in accounting hasn't done her job right, so I can't give you a budget for what you propose." That's the Blamer's way of not taking responsibility for making a decision. Nothing can get done because somebody else hasn't done his or her job. The Blamer requires a lot of manipulation if you want to win a sale.

The Leveler

My ideal, a "Tess Trueheart" with all the right attributes. She's on the rise, fast, influential, intelligent, reasonable, and amiable. She knows who she is, where she is going, and how best to get there, and will help you as readily as you help her because she's as eager as you are to further a career. The Leveler is the best sellee of the lot, a mover who's willing to make decisions, take realistic risks, be wide open to whatever you can provide that will move her ahead even faster. She will make good things happen for you because you will benefit her.

THE ART OF MAKING DATES

I think the thing that bothers me most is setting up an appointment, because I find that even with the tools I have for getting through the secretary, once I've gotten through to the person I want to talk to, he'll still resist me. He'll try to weasel out of making a date, or even make one and then cancel it. What I do is keep calling and calling. It may take weeks or months to set up an appointment, but once I get there, everything is fine. I'm sure it's just the telephone situation people resist.

They never call you back. They're always in meetings or out to lunch. I leave my number once, twice, and then I'm embarrassed to keep pestering.

Make no mistake, getting an appointment to meet with your prospect is a giant and often difficult step. Miss it and you can forget all the rest. It's easy to miss, too. Executives are harried people and their schedules don't permit making priorities of new business such as yours. What you have to do is make seeing you a priority.

DEFROSTING THE COLD CALL

I shuffle my contact cards around on my desk all day long, hating to pick up the phone and make the calls. Hating to chance getting a *No*. But I know that if I don't pick up the phone, I'll never get the appointments I must have. It's a circular agony for me.

One of the toughest of all appointments to get is when you're calling cold. It's the same as a blind date: Neither party really wants any part of it. The social caller has to find some way to break the ice and gain acceptance, usually by mentioning a mutual friend's name, a common interest, or a strong competitive edge. The same applies to a cold call in business. If you're an unknown and you want an appointment, you'd best find a way to make yourself desirable.

The call-warmer of choice is the use of a contact. "I was speaking with your friend Gail last week and she suggested I contact you about an idea I have that she believes would benefit your company." The "idea" could be in the product you sell, the service you have to offer, or the employment or assignment you want.

One of the hardest transitions to make is when you've worked for a large corporation and no longer have that credential. Being able to say, "This is Susan Brown of the Mammoth Corporation" carries a lot of weight. "This is Susan Brown" conveys little. You need the connection, so it's, "My friend Will tells me he saw you at your club last week and you mentioned you're looking for an expert fashion stylist. I've styled covers for *Mademoiselle, Vanity Fair* and ..."

Anne-Marie, a relocation expert, frequently has to make cold calls. She says that for her they're the most horrid part of the whole selling routine. Listen:

> The worst part of the selling process is the initial telephone contact. I think it's especially difficult for me because in my case the people I need to make appointments with are human resource managers. Try convincing the person on the phones that you're not looking for a job when you ask for the name of the manager. He or she invariably snaps, "We don't have any jobs. Just send in your resume."
>
> I have to keep explaining that *I* have something the human resources manager will be interested in. Most times I have to call back a half-dozen times, until I get a different assistant who will put me through.

An insurance consultant describes her experiences with cold calls this way:

> Sometimes I send a personal letter and follow it with a phone call, sometimes I do it the other way around. Either way, the letter is

really a backup for the call. Once in a while, I do a buckshot mailing and send out a letter to maybe 150 prospects. Even though I only expect one or two percent response, the letter is there and I can use it as a reason for calling. Other times, when I've just barely met someone and no real contact has been established, I'll break the ice for my phone call with a letter such as this:

Dear Ms. Jones:

That was indeed an inspiring evening at the Insurance Women's Club. I strongly believe that if Rotary Club dinner meetings work for men, they should work for us, too.

For the past 13 years I've headed the Executive Businesswoman's Division of ABC Insurance Company. We have been very successful in catering to the needs of women interested in protecting themselves and their families against loss of income. You may know some of our clients; they include Margo White, Susan Brown, Emma Green, and Betty Black—all of whom, like you, run advertising agencies.

Because I'm interested in expanding our client roster, I'm taking the liberty of attaching a brief questionnaire in the hope that either you or someone in your firm might want more information about ABC. I'm interested in doing business with women whenever possible, and hope you share this attitude.

Enclosed please find a brief description of our service, the questionnaire, and a stamped return envelope. Many thanks, in advance, for your kindness and I hope to see you again in the near future.

Cordially,

WHAT TO DO WITH THE COLD RESPONSE

Often when you're asking for an appointment you'll find yourself on the receiving end of a chilly response such as, "We're not interested." Or, "We already have your kind of service." Or, "We don't have a budget for your service." A follow-up letter can change that implied No to a "Yes, come in and see us," if it contains a hand-tailored benefit for the prospect. You can arrive at what will intrigue him or her by finding out, either through prior research or on the phone, what the company already has by way of your kind of service.

With this information, you can then offer what the prospect company lacks. If their response is "We already have some," you can state a way that you can supplement the existing service. If it's "We have no money" and your research says that they do spend but that this fiscal year is taken, you can plant seeds for the future: "I understand that you have budget limitations for this fiscal quarter. I feel, nonetheless, that it would be worth our meeting to explore the possibilities for your next fiscal year."

GETTING PAST THE SECRETARY

Sometimes the cold call doesn't get off the ground simply because you can't get past a secretary. Before you put all the blame on her or him, though, listen to what Ellen has to say:

> I've been his secretary for twenty years. I sure know how this place works, and I'd be happy to help the salespeople get appointments with the right connections—if they wouldn't be so uptight. Some of them hear a woman's voice on the other end, and I know they're thinking "dumb secretary."
>
> "I want to talk to the boss," they say to me. They see him listed in the book as head of the department and decide they'll only talk to him. He's the head of the department, but he doesn't make the buying decision. His partners do that, and I know just which ones are interested in what.
>
> Some of the women who call miss the boat, trying to sell something, calling from long distances to set up a meeting. But they make believe the call is "a personal matter." Or they say, "I'd rather talk to him directly."
>
> I figure if they don't think enough of me to inform me, then I'll take the message and let it go at that. I could really do them some good, too. But if they keep insisting that the person with a certain title is the only one who will help them, I can't worry about giving them business.
>
> There was a woman last year who really enlisted my help. She was calling from California and told me all about her product. It was fascinating but unusual. I didn't think anyone in our department would be interested, but I asked around and came up with

someone. Next time this saleswoman called, I had a name for her, and I helped her make the appointment. She made her sale, and she sent me a lovely plant for my desk—she really didn't have to—and I felt really good that it worked out so well.

As I said, it really does feel good to help other people get where they want to go.

THE SECRETARY: FRIEND OR FOE

What you get when you phone somebody for an appointment is the secretary, a.k.a. the guardian.

There are secretaries who function like Ellen above, and there is the type who plays office wife (in most cases, the secretary is a woman) and views you as a threat simply because you're another woman—somebody to be kept away from her employer and out of her daytime marriage. While her fantasy is unreal, she is real and you are going to have to deal with her. In fact, you are going to have to deal with both types.

The best way to do this is to write or fax the secretary in the same way you would approach her employer. "Mark Jones and I were discussing your company a few evenings ago, and he suggested that I see your employer, Mr. Smith, because he felt that my work would be of particular interest to your company. I'll be in your neighborhood on Wednesday and Thursday, the thirtieth and thirty-first, and I would like to make an appointment on one of those two days at Mr. Smith's convenience." Incidentally, putting the contact's name first, "Mark Jones and I," is a subtlety that adds weight, both by putting your credential up front and by introducing yourself via a name that is already familiar.

Or you can arouse the guardian's empathy: "I can't seem to get through to meet with your boss. Is he not interested in me? Or is he not interested in this kind of widget? What's the best way of getting to see him? What would you suggest we do?" The use of *we* suggests that you're in this together now. You're making the secretary feel that her help is important and that she is important. Telling her, "I know I can rely on you to get that information through. You're the only one who can really help me," lets her know that you recognize her power and invites her to exhibit it to you by following through.

Lili, a securities analyst, has learned important lessons in fielding difficult secretaries' ploys and, as a result, has succeeded in winning sales that once were lost to her. She reports, "After a year at this, I've become quite successful at selling. One thing that's helped immensely is having learned how often a secretary will try power plays. She'll say, 'I'm sorry, so-and-so is busy' or 'I can't get through to him.' I didn't know how to deal with that at first, and I wasted a lot of time just getting put off by secretaries.

"Now I play their games and try to make myself sound as important as possible so that I'll get through to the person I want. Very often, if I'm trying to make an appointment with someone and the secretary says, 'So-and-so is busy,' I'll say, 'This is the Giant Corporation calling.' Or if she says, 'So-and-so is busy and can't talk to you right now,' I'll say, 'He asked me to call and give him certain information.' I'll even lie if I have to, to get through to that person. I wouldn't have done that in the beginning. One just has to be more assertive.

"Also, I think women don't take themselves seriously if they're just starting. They think, 'Well, it's not the real thing.' You have to come to the place where you say, 'This is serious. This is a job. This is the work world and if I want to succeed I've got to play it the way it works.'"

Reality: *Selling is persistence.*

One of the greatest astonishments to the novice in selling is the exasperating number of times you may have to telephone before you actually get your prospect on the line. It can take the persistence and patience of an Alexander Graham Bell to get that "one win out of ten" that counts. A friend of mine who's a book designer recently moved east from northern New Mexico and ran up against the most frustrating experiences of her career, trying to break into the frantically paced New York market. She says:

> People just don't return phone calls here. I couldn't believe it at first, but they don't. I'd keep leaving my name and number, and I'd never hear back. I'd call the same person once, twice a week for weeks and the signal was always "He's busy. He's out. He's in conference. Call back in a week." It was so daunting.
>
> Now I've learned how to handle it. I *do* keep calling back umpteen times until I get through, and I do *not* let myself feel

put down or insulted. I realize that I'm just one of hundreds of people trying to reach the same busy executive. Out of all those pink "While You Were Out" slips piled up on his desk, the only calls he'll have time to return are the ones that look important. So, I just call as many times as it takes for him to get the cue that my call is important.

The attitude that, "I called him, now it's his turn to call me" gets you nothing but long, fruitless waits. The dripping faucet routine gets you action. Keep calling and you'll get more appointments. Get more appointments and you'll get more sales. It's simply a matter of statistics again.

Reality: *If you can't make an appointment, you can't make a sale. The art of making appointments is a basic in the art of selling.*

"I COULD SCREAM EVERY TIME I *LOOK* AT A PHONE"

Connecting by telephone in the late 1990s brings with it something old—or at least familiar—and something new. What's old is that jittery feeling before and during making a business call, and what's new is that with all the technology monitoring the phone lines, you're lucky if you speak to a real person the first time around.

Let's start with your attitude about phoning:

If it's hard for you, write yourself a script in advance, so you'll know what you want to say, and say it. You can lose track and control by winging phone conversations. Rehearse your script, too, so you'll hear how it sounds and be comfortable with it when you're actually on the phone. "Good morning, Mr. Smith. John Jones suggested I call to make an appointment with you. He feels that my style of work as a professional fashion photographer is exactly what you're looking for right now."

Plan the time you'll be on the phone for only a minute or two. In New York that's all you're going to get. In smaller towns and other parts of the country, the pace is a bit more leisurely and you'll be encouraged to insert pleasantries and asides. Go right ahead and make the most of the getting-to-know-you opportunity—but do it quickly and keep in mind that your goal is to get an appointment because you have something beneficial to offer. You want a *Yes* to your request, or at least a *No*. Never let your prospect ramble off with a *Maybe*. Make sure the cycle's completed.

If you have so large a number of phone calls to make that the very idea is fazing, slice the number into segments: eight on Monday, eight on Tuesday, and so on until the list is completed and you've reached your goal. Completing that telephone cycle will permit you to go on to the next set of goals on your agenda. If it happens that Tuesday is a poor day for you, don't worry about making the eight calls that day. Just crank them into other days; what's important is that you meet your end deadline.

Two more bits of advice. One: If you've already explored and have the information you need, use or consider hiring an assistant to make the appointments for you. Having somebody whose time is less valuable than yours do the phoning saves you time, money, and the annoyance of having to do groundwork you don't savor.

And two: Telephone with a positive attitude, and the response you get will more likely be positive, too. Always assume that the person you are calling has been waiting to hear about the benefit you're about to offer.

What's new? The electronic gatekeepers, who are becoming ever more universal! A friend of mine recently returned to New York after living in Japan for four years. I asked him what the biggest difference he noticed was and he said, "No live bodies." He may be in for a great surprise as he settles into the course of American business communications. We're not too far from "no live bodies," either. That is, you get on the phone and you reach someone else's phone—it's all equipment, messages being channeled from one electronic message center to another. As you try to get through to someone, hours can pass.

How to deal with it? Years ago, a secretary or titled assistant acted as gatekeeper for the executive in charge. You learned a few ways in or around them. For example, you learned he answered his own phones before nine in the morning, but not after five in the afternoon, when his keepers were not around. Or, you could become friendly with the secretary or assistant so she'd put you right through, or at least be sure that your message was on the top of the list.

Today, with voice mail on most phone extensions at work, even the gatekeepers have electronic gatekeepers. How do you interact with the answering machine? *Make it quick*—do not leave lengthy messages; state why you're calling and ask to be advised if you've reached the right person, so you can get an immediate response.

The same rule holds true for E-mail communication. One of the problems CEOs and other executives are experiencing is the abuse of on-line connections—people merrily sending lengthy bulletins they don't have time to read. Because an executive has an E-mail address, don't take up volumes of space getting your message to him or her—it's poor etiquette and it won't attract anyone to your business concerns. *Be cryptic* and take action by sending an E-mail that succinctly describes your message. You might even ask the executive to check off a "yes-no" answer or set up an options list. Remember, if you would not necessarily call the CEO on her direct line, don't E-mail her with volumes of information she will not pay attention to.

YOUR PROSPECT'S ON THE PHONE. WHAT DO YOU SAY TO GET THE APPOINTMENT?

You get attention and arouse interest and desire fast. If you have a contact, always lead with it: "Mr. Jones, Charlie Contact suggested I call you ..." Or, lacking the contact, find another connection: "I saw an item in the *Wall Street Journal* about the problem you're having currently with your lawsuit and I have some information I believe would help you. I'd like to come see you this Wednesday or Thursday to discuss it. Which day would be better for you?" Use this approach only if you are very sure of your facts, when you have an inside line and know what you have is what they're looking for. Otherwise, you're going to waste your time and infuriate your would-be customer.

What you're doing is putting your benefit up front, without giving it all away, and then limiting his or her choices to when, not if, he or she will see you. "I'll be in your neighborhood Wednesday and Thursday. Which is better for you? ... You can't make it this week? How about next week on Monday or Tuesday?"

WHEN NOT TO MAKE AN APPOINTMENT

But before you say Monday or Tuesday, find out if it's going to be worth your while and what you should bring with you by asking questions. If your exploration reveals that you've nothing to win by making an appointment, don't. As a magazine space saleswoman puts it, "I never force an appointment until I know what the budget is."

When you get the date you want, I'm sure you're aware that your tone of voice will have had something to do with it. Enthusiasm and sincerity come through as unmistakably and contagiously by phone as they do in person. The difference is, on the phone you don't have the confirming underscore of facial expression or body language. That's why successful people consciously practice projecting a good telephone voice.

SELLING WHEN THE PRODUCT IS YOU

When I'm selling myself, I'm always anxious because I always have to make sure I'm making a positive self-presentation. In essence, what I'm selling is trust. I'm also selling the information and skills that I have to give, but I'm really selling trust. It causes me a lot of anxiety because I'm really on the line and very vulnerable.

Today, tomorrow, any number of times in your career you're going to face the awesome mission of getting yourself a job, a raise, a promotion, or an increase in rates for what you do. If you're normal, you'll black out. "This isn't selling," you'll say. "This is different. It's me—taking a step *toward* selling. First I get the job or promotion, then I have something to sell."

Right, and wrong. Yes, it *is* you. No, it isn't different; you're selling from first to last. Because selling is how you will get a job or raise, a promotion or fee increase. You'll use exactly the same attitude and abilities as when you sell a product or service. In both circumstances, what you are doing is persuading, influencing, or manipulating people into wanting to buy what you have. The only difference, if it helps you to look at it as a difference, is that when no product is involved, you're persuading people to buy *your ability to fill a need*. Your skills are the product—in other words, the product is you. And selling yourself, your ability to fill a need, demands proficiency and knowledge identical to selling land, baby food, or wash-off tattoos.

Reality: *Selling is selling, whether it's yourself or a product.*

WHAT DO YOU WANT AND WHY DO YOU WANT IT?

Step back and examine your realities. What are you shooting for, exactly, and is it a reasonable target for you at this point? Is the change one you can afford? How will the job, raise, or promotion advance your career and move you toward your long-range goals? Have you put a timetable on completing your objective? Now is the time, at the outset, to make sure you're not hacking away haphazardly at an endeavor that may not be appropriate for you. Ask yourself tough questions and come to concrete conclusions. Begin here:

- Where are you now in your career?
- Where can it lead if you stay there?
- What's in it for you if you shift gears into another career?
- What do you want that necessitates change? Why or how will change be an improvement?
- Is it possible for you to stay at your company or do you realistically expect another round of downsizing?
- Is this field, company, or partner competitive any longer, or is it time to switch?

THINK IN SPECIFICS

Say you've been a junior loan officer at a bank for three years; now you've got your eye on a promotion to head loan officer. Why do you want the job? Because it seems a natural progression? Your friends will think more of you? It means more money? You're aiming at the bank manager's job? Is the promotion a requirement to move into a department that interests you more, for example, foreign loans and international banking?

Be clear on your real motivation. Is banking what you want to stay with, or do you have a stronger affinity? Should you use your position at the bank to get experience in accounting rather than loans?

If another field beckons, is this the right time to move into it? Have you accrued enough knowledge and accreditation to move on? Is the grass really greener over there or will the economics, the opportunities, the corporate game set you up to hit a glass ceiling?

DON'T MAKE A MOVE UNTIL YOU RESEARCH IT

If you want to stay out of trouble, avert mistakes, and be effective in whatever you do professionally or personally, assume nothing, ever. When the car in front of you speeds up, you don't assume the light has turned green. You take a moment and check it out for yourself. When you find the perfect apartment, you don't assume utilities are included in the rent. You ask about all the costs in detail. Just so, when you decide you want a job, a raise, a promotion, or an increase in your rates, dig in and get all the facts before you barge ahead.

I repeat, with emphasis: *Assume nothing, ever.*

RESEARCH THE TERRAIN

One of the first things you'll want to find out is what possibilities are open to you in your field of interest. Be specific. You'll need to learn everything you can about the market, the competition, the industry as a whole, and the product or services in particular. Ascertain who makes and influences the decision to buy what you have to offer. Find out who your competition is, what qualifications you need, what your prospect is looking for. Learn the field and the company: What's the target market, what are the objectives and the goals? What is your prospect's competitive advantage and how can yours fit in with it? Do you see an interesting way to expand the market?

Explore what the general trends are and how you can help your prospect lead the competition. If certain tools such as writing a proposal or a contract are foreign to you, ask somebody to show you how to do it. Never be afraid to ask questions, even when you're being interviewed. Your interest and intelligence will be noted and appreciated. Nobody expects you to be Wonder Woman with all the answers, and you can err disastrously by making assumptions, by guessing rather than being up-front.

You never outgrow your need for research, no matter what stage you're at—on the climb or an old pro. Research means talking to friends, colleagues, anybody in or out of the business whom you can buttonhole to supply information. It means attending organization dinners and seminars, belonging to trade associations to keep on top of what's going on, making contacts, learning what other successful people have done. It means keeping up with what's what and who's who through business publications, books, brochures, company reports on and off the Internet—every relevant "byte" of information you can get your hands on. Listen for buzzwords and ideas, pick up information about corporate philosophy and self-image, and explore the company's and the field's current financial picture and its potential for expansion.

Cultivate at least four good sources for gossip, to stay in the know: who's been fired, what new business is breaking, where things are opening up. Lunch out often, throw cocktail parties, make a point of swapping shoptalk. Get in on the gossip network and you're in on the latest news on the wire.

THE CASE OF A SUCCESSFUL RESEARCHER

Anne-Marie is a French-born woman who specializes in relocating people whose companies—her clients—regularly transfer executives and their families from other countries to Atlanta. Her services provide a means of easing the transition by helping to locate appropriate housing, schools, transportation, physicians, cultural amenities, and so on.

Anne-Marie went into business for herself three years ago, but not until she'd done thorough preliminary research to find out whether it was a profitable idea or not. She checked out other relocation companies in Atlanta, talked with them and their clients, read trade publications, got government statistics and information from every available source. She learned how many competitors she would have; what she could offer that they could not; how many prospects she could realistically turn into clients; and what her fees should be, based on overhead and the going rates.

Before Anne-Marie could go out and sell her services she needed to find the clients who could buy them. So her next "locating" job was for herself: She researched the marketplace for likely prospects. In her words, here is exactly how she went about it:

How do I find the companies who need my services? I know that they have to be international; I've staked my competitive advantage on the fact that I'm multilingual. I know I'm seeking major corporations, with the money to spend on personnel transfers. And I know they have to have an office in Atlanta, where I operate.

So I started with the Fortune 500 and 100 lists and found the companies with both foreign offices and one in Atlanta. I also used a few of the other specialized business directories; there's one for every field at the library.

Another way to do research on your prospects, especially if you're looking for a job, is to have exploratory interviews with minor companies in your field of interest. Never do this with the key ones; you save those for the sell. I'd want to learn what people in relocation need, and I'd want to pick up whatever contacts I could, too.

A good approach, I've found, is not to apply for a job but to call on another matter. For example, I take a lot of continuing education courses and I could assign myself a paper to explore the industry. Or, since I like to write, I could find a publication that needs a story and ask somebody for an interview. Or I could teach a course and invite people who interest me to be guest speakers.

I may not always be in business for myself. I could work for another company—and I'll go about finding who needs me the same way I find my own clients. I'll look up which relocation companies have offices in Atlanta and concentrate on those with an international clientele. I'll research them in ways that I need to know about them as an employee—using my contacts—and learn what companies need, what they lack. I'll find out what their "corporate culture" is—the tone of the place—so I won't make the mistake of trying to fit into a company that's wrong for me.

Arm yourself to the teeth with all the information you can plug into!

Reality: *Homework in depth always pays off.*

BE HARDHEADED

Are you committed enough to put a deadline on your move and stick to it? Have you written down a schedule, a goal timetable? Putting off job hunts and interviews is both alluring and self-destructive—and procrastination can trap you. Rationalization that says, "One of these days I'll really do something about it," is much easier than getting out there and hustling. Or wrestling the enemy and facing fear of rejection. Be willing to follow through and get what you want!

PAY YOUR DUES

Finally, are you willing to give up something as well as to gain? There's a trade-off for everything. That's something you have to accept, going in. If you want a face-lift you must accept having tiny scars. If you want a job in Chicago, you'll have to leave your house and friends in Dubuque. If you want to sell your first song, TV script, or novel, you'll have to give up your dream of a million-dollar first-time sale in exchange for creating a track record, breaking in at a lower fee, but making the difference in your career.

When I ran my market research company, in the beginning years, we were willing to take jobs we knew we'd lose money on, as a trade-off for gaining credibility and muscle in fields that were new to us.

Marian's is a story about trade-offs for validation that may ring a bell for you. She'd reached the point where she could leave her career of wife and mother and get into the business world. Never having worked, her skills were limited. But there was one thing she liked and was good at: cooking. Marian decided she wanted to work for one of the gourmet-chef cooking schools in her city.

First she sent out resumes but, lacking professional credentials, that effort netted nothing. So she lowered the bar and offered her services as an unpaid apprentice. She telephoned cooking school chef after chef, saying: "I'll sweep your floors and scrub your pots if you'll give me the opportunity to sit at your feet." Her offer hit home with one of the chefs and for six months Marian chopped garlic, peeled vegetables, cleaned pots, and observed the maestro at work.

Then one day she found herself in the familiar leading-lady-breaks-a-leg situation. The chef became ill just before a demonstration and suddenly Marian was the only suitable stand-in for the star. There she was, the school's sole available teacher of the chef's specialty: dessert souffles.

Naturally, she killed herself getting the recipe perfect, mimicking every technique she'd seen the chef employ—and reading cookbooks by chefs she respected for extra ideas on the subject. She worked as good-humoredly and expertly as Julia Child would have done, teaching techniques to the class—a great milestone experience for her.

When the chef returned, Marian approached him. She said, "Now I know that I'm able to teach desserts, and do it well, and no longer want to be your kitchen assistant. I want my own class to instruct. If you have doubts, I'll prove to you that I really have done a great job."

The proof was in letters of commendation Marian asked her satisfied students to send to the chef. They were her accreditation and because of them, Marian got her own class. The six months she had labored as scullery maid were her dues-paying trade-off for the validation that enabled her to get the job she really wanted.

WHERE TO FIND A JOB

There are three basic sources for job hunters: ads, employment services, and contacts. The greatest of these is contacts.

Newspaper ads are probably the poorest way to find a job. Most of the good jobs are taken quickly by people who hear about them through the gossip-and-contact network, or they are filled from within. When good jobs are advertised in the paper, there's a slew of competition for them. Not to say that a lot of good jobs aren't found by following the ads; they are. But a lot of better jobs are never advertised at all.

Employment agencies and executive searchers are fine, but they have their drawbacks, too. As middlemen and women, searchers may not always have the correct information, or they may screen you out because you don't fit into their written job descriptions. It's much easier for them to work with people who can be readily pigeonholed, people who are ready-made matchups with job specifications. If you're changing fields, a great deal of creative thought and work may have to go into categorizing you so you can be placed in a waiting pigeonhole.

Your best bet, when you're looking for a job or assignment, a raise or promotion, is *contacts*. Use them! Advertise your needs. Talk to people—with appropriate discretion, of course. If you're on the job, you want to keep the atmosphere pleasant until you actually move on. There are ways to get the word out without putting your head on the block: Have your contacts with influence or information put you in touch with the right people. And, if you remember the Rule of Three, each person you mention your needs to will become a support system of people who can help you fill them.

Perhaps you know months ahead that you're going to leave your job. Emily had that experience: She told her employer eight weeks in advance that she wanted to further her career by getting into an allied field. She was lucky, too. For those few months she had the encouragement—and the names of contacts she'd gotten from at least half the people in the office. It was an enormously helpful way to find the job that was right for her.

The contacts you reach out to can put you in touch with a potential employer, but no one can guarantee that you'll get the job. That's up to you, your research, and how well you use it. An instance came up when I had my market research company that I'd like to pass along to you because the follow-through was so imaginative.

A friend had called and asked me to see Ginny, a young woman he'd met at a trade show. Because of the contact, I made the appointment—I'll always make time for somebody when there's a friend's name attached. Ginny turned out to be personable but inexperienced, and there was no trainee slot in my company where she could be placed. However, she showed such enthusiasm and came with so many good ideas that I said *Yes* to three more meetings.

At each meeting Ginny would ask questions about the company and the industry. Then she'd go out, do some research, and call me back with ideas and solutions. She was doing my work for me, and doing it well. She became so valuable that she created a position for herself. I hired her three months after meeting her.

A young man told me how research paid off for him. Dan is a skilled language workshop leader and had the idea of selling his ability to a local university. He said:

> I went out to the college to find out who needed workshops and discovered I had a lot of competition in the language department. I'd be just one more person begging for a job if I stayed in that niche. So I dug in to find out the best way to present myself.
>
> I met with some thirty different people—professors, students, secretaries—and learned from my survey that the competition for jobs was among the salaried professors. That meant I should approach the continuing education department, where they let you try anything if it'll attract student enrollment.
>
> I worked up a proposal for the department head and assured him that I knew from research that the community needed language workshops, and that I personally knew ten people who would enroll. I told him I was confident I could get together a system that would keep people coming in. I also set it up so he'd have nothing to lose.
>
> He was concerned about the cost of advertising the workshop. I said, "You don't have to advertise because I want to start the course in two weeks, I had enough names of potential students anyway, so the advertising wouldn't make any difference." It worked.
>
> I didn't come in asking for a job, I came in with an attractive plan that didn't cost the department anything. I got what I wanted and the workshops have been very successful.

THE INVENT-A-NICHE METHOD

A fourth and superb source for getting a job or a promotion is to see or create a need, and then fill it. Here are a couple of situations that will activate your imagination so you can devise programs of your own.

Assume you're a secretary at Survey & Analysis, Inc. It's a young corporation and on the grow. So are you, and what you want to build is a career, not just a job. Your next goal is to move up within S & A, Inc., but at this stage in its growth the company must limit its personnel and there are no vacant slots you might fill. So, create one.

To begin, you study and analyze the organization and its problems. As a secretary, you're in a position to see that the firm is in a tight financial position and that one way to reduce overhead would be to investigate using alternate suppliers. On your own, you conduct the appropriate research and then present your findings to the president. You offer to effect continued savings in return for the heretofore nonexistent duties and salary of office manager.

Take another situation. For three years you have done a creditable job as account executive at an advertising agency. You want to move up. So, through a contact, you bring in a new client whose cosmetics business is one the agency's not dealt with before. You understand the cosmetics business, having researched the field, and furthermore the new client is personally cemented to you. You explain to the agency president the size of the new client's budget, its immediate profit and its potential, and how handling the account will attract additional clients from other areas of the women's products field. What you ask for in exchange for bringing in a valuable new client is the *title* and *salary* of "account supervisor of beauty and fashion"—a new division of the company you've just invented.

In both of these scenarios you have observed a need and then devised a means to fulfill it. You have gotten your promotion by selling a product: *yourself and your ability to fill a need.* If you think about it, you have called upon your life experience as a woman, transferring your ability to empathize with friends to your employer: "I appreciate what you need, and I understand your problem; now I'd like you to consider my solution."

FIND A NEED AND FILL IT

The founder of Buckeye Beans, a former artist and potter, began her small business by packaging delicious soup mixes for busy working women in cheery bags with charmingly written instructions. She got to love her business; she went to food trade shows and looked around, thinking where her company could go next. Her choice? She expanded into the pasta market by thinking *novelty*—that is, she marketed *theme* pasta. Bags of colored pasta shaped like baseballs and bats, golf clubs, Christmas trees and sea-sonally related shapes, fruits and veggies, you name it. If you think there's no new way to make a noodle, look at Buckeye Beans. The company is phenomenally successful because the owner asked herself the right questions about finding and creating her niche, bringing the right person in (her husband, as it turned out) to help market and expand the business further. She was a smart entre-preneur who found her way into a huge and internationally com-petitive market.

Then there's Diane, who's more than a fashion designer; she is an entrepreneurial designer, with a lot of "fire in the belly." Diane didn't shift occupations, going from pots to beans, but stayed in fashion. She had many role models who'd come through the ranks in the garment center and gone on to have their own companies, such as Donna Karan. She wanted the same success.

As she put it, "I don't want to ride home in somebody else's cab. I'm not content just to design clothes that others put under their label. I'm managerial. I want to run my own business, write my own rules, make a name for myself, and do it on my terms."

A year ago Diane was working as a designer for a company that had a make-it-or-break-it season—the spring line would either put them on the fashion map or wipe them out. It was that tight a sit-uation. Both partners liked Diane's designs and saw her as ripe ma-terial for head designer—and the reviews and sales of the upcom-ing show would tell. But they wanted her backstage. No name on the label, as in Diane Designs for Ragtrade Juniors.

What Diane wanted was to come center stage and start building her own design studio. She thought, "The timing is great—it's right now. I hold 90 percent of the cards. Without my designs they can't possibly produce the spring line in time, nor can they replace me and get the line out and on the runway. This is a wonderful opportunity for me to come up with a plan that's to their advantage and mine."

Diane could have gone in and put a gun to her bosses' heads, threatening to pull out unless they set her up with a design studio she could manage. That would have created hostility and gotten her no further than springtime. Instead, she researched the firm's needs very carefully, to see how she could sweeten the pot for the partners while getting what she wanted.

Diane came up with a meticulously itemized proposal. It encompassed a design fee and percentage of the gross for herself, and included the costs of leasing and setting up a separate studio, payroll, fabric, and a reasonable budget for the launch party; she included the number of designs she would produce per season, and the time required. She explained to the partners how their investment in her would be to the company's advantage. She would take care of locating and leasing the space, pull together her production staff (cutter, grader, sewing machine operators, etc.), and work out all the administrative details, working with their accountant and lawyer. This would free the partners of the groundwork of a new undertaking. She added:

> It also allowed us to work together in a new way. Before, when I was on their payroll, we were not dealing with each other as equals. I was just an employee. Now they began to take me seriously, to see me as much in a management capacity as in design.

Diane had her lawyer draw up a contract, with a payout schedule that wouldn't place the company in a bind while she could still realize a profit. That flexibility on her part also helped win her bosses' agreement to finance her studio.

I should say, "her former bosses' agreement." Diane and they are now peers professionally. She's running Diane Designs while Ragtrade handles sales and distribution of the line—a complete win–win situation.

THE BIG HANG-UP: ASKING FOR WHAT YOU WANT

Herein lies the rub in all our selling efforts, most especially when what we're selling is ourselves. Asking for a job, a raise, or anything else we want is painfully difficult. It's the one thing we don't know how to do, and resist doing by reflex. Asking is antithetical to nearly everything we've learned as women, and the one area where we have a small backlog of experience we can transfer to a business skill.

Everything else is there: giving people what they want, listening to what they say and don't say, reacting to situations, organizing projects, persuading. But when it comes to asking for something for ourselves, we have nothing we can convert into selling ability. What we know from conditioning—although it's changed a lot in the last 20 years—is that women are to be givers who wait to be given, and, therefore, it would be wrong or intrusive to express our own needs.

Although these generational differences are not 100 percent descriptive of each group, and there's lots of overlapping of traits, in general this is what we see in the business world: Women over 45 are especially affected by the old pre-feminist rules to pull back and let others have their way. They were trained by their mothers (and social codes of the time) to be oblique and never direct, to be coy, "feminine," and teasing or a study in passive-aggression. Women under 45 got mixed messages and were told: "Ask for it—you deserve it" but with an undercurrent of doubt that told them, counterproductively, "Don't dare ask for it—they'll laugh in your face."

As a result, some women simply retreat in panic from asking for anything, worrying, "What if they say *No*? ... It's better never to ask than to ask for something and not get it, or worse, to be despised for having asked."

Women in their 20s and 30s are more direct—they grew up with sexual politics and mothers who made the tiny gains, step by step, in the workforce. These women are used to asking for what they want, less likely to be afraid of not getting it or of being called unfeminine, and not as confused about mixed messages.

If it will help you to end your hang-up about asking, stop polarizing certain attributes as "masculine" (for example, pursuing what you want outside the home) or "feminine" (that is, pursuing what you want inside the home) and applying judgments to them. There are differences between men and women, some hormonally attributable, some environmentally influenced, some genetically acquired—truths about the sexes that cannot be disputed. John Gray was right in much of what he said about sex differences in his book, *Men Are from Mars, Women Are from Venus*.

However, when we are talking about the economic realities of the workplace—having a career plan, being focused, and going after it—you must put certain attitudes about males and females to the side, or they will keep you back.

If it will help, neuter the attribute and desexualize it—*A goal has no gender.* If you want something, figure out where it is and how to get it, and ask for it.

Reality: *Statistics say you will have at least four to six careers and you must sell yourself each time. Selling is asking.*

THE MYTH OF ASKING BY MAGIC

How often have you heard someone complain, "I'm so angry with that man! I've killed myself for him for three years and never once has he given me a raise. You'd think he could see for himself that I should be paid more for the hard work I do."

Sure he should. But how does he know? All he does is sign the paychecks on Fridays, he doesn't evaluate each one. And he's not your mommy, who was so sensitive to your wants she always gave whatever was in your mind before you had to ask for it. In other words, you have to let people know what you want if you want to get it. Believing that you don't have to ask just because you hate asking is believing in magic, an illusion that's all smoke. The reality is, *not asking means not getting.* And not getting leads to brooding, and brooding leads to being angry because somebody didn't do what you secretly wanted them to do. Asking by magic—who needs it?

If you don't ask for what you want, unless you're working with Kreskin, a professional mind reader, you're never going to get it. Practice is needed.

THE BIGGEST HANG-UP: ASKING FOR MONEY

"Money is dirty stuff ... The love of money is the root of all evil ... Women never discuss money ... Finances are a man's job ... Cash is hard, women are soft." So goes the old litany, still influencing women as we near the year 2000—women who are appalled when they have to ask for money for what they do. That's what prostitutes do, they think—cash up front exchanged for a service. But money *does* count, and if you want it, it's a topic you must tackle, resolve, and become comfortable with once and for all.

You need to change your thinking from, "Clean money is the money I get from my father, my mother, or my husband; dirty money is the money I have to ask for myself." When you do, you can reach the stage Vicki did when she finally got a solid career going. She said:

> It's heaven to be getting the money I deserve every week. For the first time I can do things for myself: take myself to dinner, furnish my apartment, buy clothes, have the things I need and the luxuries I don't need at all. And I don't have to depend on anyone else to do these things for me.

Reality: *Selling usually is about money.*

Money is business. It is the measure of the quality of wares and services. It is what changes hands in nearly all transactions, the end result of the selling process. Get used to the facts and make friends with them. Money is your friend, and it's what selling is usually all about. It signals the worth of your abilities, the extent to which you are in charge of yourself and situations. It bespeaks initiative and professionalism.

Money is power and to be timid about asking for it is to automatically preclude advancement in your career. A job, a raise, a promotion, all the steps that mark you as a person of value carry with them the symbol of money. Unless you take money into account and become comfortable asking for what you are worth, that symbol and its ancillary benefits will not be conferred upon you.

Two points of view may help you become comfortable. One is that asking for money is nothing more than the barter system at work. It is what you receive in exchange for filling a need that somebody has. Barter is not aggressive or pushy or nasty. It is a kindly exchange, a safe and productive reality. And reality is the coin of every successful person.

The second way to make peace with asking for your money is to change the language in your head, translating *ask* to *offer*. When you ask for what you want, whether it's the signature on a sales contract or a raise, you are pointing out what you have and offering to provide it. You are saying, in effect, "I can plan, organize, and meet deadlines so expertly that your profits will increase if you accept my offer to put those abilities to work for you. In exchange, I expect you to reciprocate and compensate me for value received."

Reality: *If you don't ask for what you are worth, you probably won't get it.*

One of the problems I keep hearing voiced is the one Julie expresses as an anxiety. She said:

I get anxious about naming my price. I'm afraid to say to somebody, "No, I want more." What's worse is trying to come to terms in my mind with what my price is and what they will pay. I'm scared they'll tell me, "No, we've decided we don't want you at all."

In general, women don't charge what they're worth. As you know, that's a major issue that the women's movement is still addressing after 20 years: equal pay for equal work. But the law won't cover everything for you. You have to have the courage to ask even if you're feeling scared and uncomfortable. *Learn to acknowledge your worth despite your fear of asking for it.*

Until you come to grips with the fact that you deserve to be compensated and that it's your right to ask for the money you earn, you'll keep giving out signals of unworthiness. Saying things like, "I think I deserve to be paid $400?" instantly betrays your uncertainty. Omit the "I think," don't end your sentence with an inflection that goes up in tone, as if you're asking a question. Make your statement positive and sure. Drop the little-girl style. It's another clue that you're easy to get the better of, a signal people will take advantage of. Even a letter can tell tales about you. Here's a classic from the file marked, "Walking Out of the Room Backwards."

Virginia told me which apron you'd like to have. I can put it straight "into production" and have it by the 24th for you. To make it easier for me, I ask people I deal with directly to please send a check before I send the apron so I don't have to hassle bills because I only deal with shops as a rule—and try to maintain a hard business attitude.

The apron is $15 from me, but $25 plus tax at Saks, and *naturally* if you have a problem about it, it's all adjustable ... good neighbor policy!

"To make it easier for me," "so I don't have to hassle bills"—is this woman in business or apologizing for making aprons? Talk straight! Look at that "naturally": Did you ever see such a giveaway? All those flowery trills mean she just can't bear the idea of money. A real pushover.

Difficulty in acknowledging one's worth in money goes back to the social conditioning that tells us, falsely, that women are nice, money is not nice, and it's embarrassing to take money for what you do. Women have tended, therefore, to ask only for the bare necessities, enough to pay the rent, grocery, and transportation bills but not enough to pay for their time and expertise. The plain business facts are these:

1. The economic system is structured so that time and talent have cash value. Rates and salaries depend on the value of your abilities and the time you devote to a job. As your proven track record for excellence becomes stronger, your value becomes greater and so do the sums you charge. Being timid about asking for what you are worth can only lead to dealing forever with the bargain hunters of the world, nickel-and-diming yourself to the poorhouse.

    Sharon learned that lesson fairly early in her career as a marketing consultant. She'd established herself as a fund adviser whose recommendations made money for the six or eight companies that had engaged her. When a large corporation called on her to consult on a major new program, Sharon knew her $200-a-day fee was no longer appropriate. "If I charge $400, will they pay it or hire somebody else? It seems so bold to ask for so much money. I'll ask my accountant what he thinks I should do." The accountant thought she should be locked up. He pointed out, "You've proved that you're worth a lot of money to the companies that take your advice, and this one has already signaled that they believe in investing in your services. At this stage you ought to be setting your rates at $400 a day minimum, and escalate after that."

He was right: Nobody questioned the $400 fee and Sharon has since built a roster of high-paying clients who appreciate her worth and are willing to pay for what she does.

2. As you become stronger in your expertise and charge for it accordingly, you enhance your position because you are advertising that you are special and hard to get. In the same way that only a rich and discriminating few can pay for the superior model of Rolls Royce, there is cachet in your high-priced superiority. It's the same premise on which "the most expensive perfume in the world" is sold to a willing clientele over similarly excellent products.

When Hyatt Associates, my company, gives seminars for people in marketing, I've found that offering the sessions as a free service results in a reserved audience. There's an attitude that "you get what you pay for." But when I charge for the seminars, the fee automatically signals that we are authorities and people pay attention to what we say.

You don't lose sales or jobs by charging what you are worth. You build up a good reputation by dealing from your strength. All you have to lose are the jobs that cost you money.

3. Set your price realistically, and if it's higher than your prospect thinks he or she can afford, you have to be willing to hear *No*. With a *No* you can then either negotiate to a price you can live with or go on to sell your ability to another person. The point is not to fear asking what you're worth because you anticipate and dread losing the sale, and not to be stampeded into underselling yourself at bargain-basement rates. Either approach makes you a loser.

You're apt to lose, too, if you're a high-priced achiever and settle into one of the traditional low-paying and crowded women's fields such as education, health care, merchandising, or publishing. From my own experience, I can tell you that there are profitable ways to transfer your skills into a higher-paying field. In the early 1960s my career was teaching improvisation to children at community centers and summer camps. The going rate was five dollars an hour, and that's what I got.

Later in the 60s I brought the same skills to the business world. I called what I did for a living "market research," added a professional aspect by teaming up with a market researcher, and began earning the $125 hourly rate that the industry willingly paid in those years. The skills I used were identical; it was simply a matter of transferring them to where the grass was greener. My fees, of course, have gone up accordingly over the years—my experience and successes in the field reflect that.

Anybody can do the same. If your ability is in sales and you have a real affinity for selling, you can sell pharmaceuticals as well as you can sell video games. I know a woman who started as a department store cosmetics salesperson and who moved her skills and affinity into new product development for a cosmetics manufacturer. Another acquaintance who had been a low-salaried operating-room assistant transferred her expertise and interest in health care to the high-paying area of consultancy in hospital management and developmental planning. All you need is to focus on your ability, make a connection to affinities, add a bit of imagination, and move ahead on your willingness to experiment.

HOW TO PRICE YOURSELF RIGHT

Establishing what you are worth can be done in a variety of ways. Ask around. Read want ads in the newspapers and check trade journals. Research in every way possible to find out the going rates or salaries in the field you're interested in, at your level of accomplishment. There are dozens of clues to current market value. If you're in a free-lance or service field where there is little or no industry documentation, ask both buyers and sellers what the going rate is in your part of the country. Keep in mind, though, that rates change from time to time and that some people you ask may have reason to shade their responses.

Be flexible, but within limits. And set those limits, mentally, before you go and ask for the job or the raise. Ask yourself, What do I think I should be paid for this, and what's the least I will accept? Then you will be prepared to negotiate from your initial offering, if need be, but will not find yourself discounting your price below a realistic rock bottom.

If you do get into negotiation and your primary goal is the money, be prepared to lose or refuse a job if the price is too low for what your ability is worth. Just be sure, going in, that if you don't win the sale you have someplace else to go, or have enough money in the bank to tide you over. That's a super position to be in because you come from the greatest possible strength when it's absolutely all right for you to lose.

HOW TO ASK FOR WHAT YOU WANT: CLEARLY AND WITH CONFIDENCE

To communicate what you want effectively, stay on goal. Stay clear of hidden motivations such as seeking approval, and abandon counterproductive behavior such as avoiding conflict or rejection.

THE DOS OF ASKING

- Be direct. Ask for what you want without beating around the bush or watering down your message with irrelevant issues.

- Be clear. Ask for what you want specifically—so many dollars or such and such a position—and back your request with clearly perceivable reasons why granting it would be mutually favorable.

- Be calm. Apologetic, nervous giggles; distracting, jerky gestures; a tense voice and tentative inflection all negate what you want to communicate.

- Rehearse before you ask. Role-play with a partner, so that you're comfortable in the scene you're about to enter and have command of the scenario. Think of yourself as an actor about to appear before a first-night audience and prepare by practicing all the lines and gestures. Let your partner play the devil's advocate, so you'll be prepared for the objections that may arise.

Good preparation makes it easier to make that good first impression, and this is the *you* your prospect will either applaud or walk out on. You can go back again if you blow the first meeting, but it's the hard way.

The Don'ts of Asking

- Don't apologize or downplay yourself. ("I'm sorry to take up your time with something unimportant ...")

- Don't obfuscate your goal. ("I came to ask for a promotion up to head buyer but maybe you think I should be at a branch store.")

- Don't stray from your agenda. ("I want to take three weeks instead of two for my vacation. By the way, did I show you the snapshots I took two years ago when I was in Hawaii?")

- Don't clown or neutralize what you say out of nervousness. ("Uh, I want to talk with you about my salary, ha-ha-ha.")

- Don't be sexually suggestive. ("Why don't we talk about the promotion somewhere more ... interesting.")

THE SELLING GAME DO AND DON'T PLAYHOUSE

Here are two scenes from a play called *Yours for the Asking*. The show will never hit Broadway—in fact, it'll never get out of this book. The dialogues exist only to illustrate some of the dos and don'ts of asking.

SCENE I.   A new division is being formed by your company. You want to be the director, so you will rehearse one of these three scripts.

DIALOGUE A: Umm, I wouldn't turn down the opportunity of being director. I'd be willing to work in the new division if you can find somebody to cover what I do now.

DIALOGUE B: I guess I'd be interested in heading the division. If I could make the time. It's sort of related to what I do now, isn't it? I suppose it would be a good challenge for me.

DIALOGUE C: I am extremely enthusiastic about what this division will be doing. I've had a lot of experience in work of this sort, and know a lot of people in the field who can assist us in performing the work. In fact, one of the key men at our major financial resource is a friend of mine and he has already told me that he will cooperate with me on seeing that the division is successful. Also, I know that I work well with the staff here; you've commented yourself how productivity and morale have gone up since I've been in charge of the department where I am now. At this point, I could readily train somebody to take over my responsibilities at the same time I'm helping to start up the new division. I know I could help you do this thing right, and I'd really like to take on the directorship.

SCENE II.

You are applying for a job you want but you're not sure if the salary being offered is reasonable for your worth and your needs. You want to earn $35,000.

DIALOGUE A:

Well, to take the job I'd have to get more than the $25,000 I'm earning now.

DIALOGUE B:

I hate to sound pushy, but I have to know about the salary before I can decide to work for you. I couldn't take a job for less than ... how does $30,000 or $35,000 sound to you?

DIALOGUE C:

To assume the responsibilities you've outlined, I'd have to be paid enough to make it worthwhile for me to leave my present job. I've built up a lot of credentials there and in prior positions, and have shown that I can do the kind of work we're talking about, expertly and profitably. I know the value of my ability and the extent of your needs. They match beautifully. At $35,000 we could work together very well.

Curtain

[Director, enters stage left. Holds large placard to audience.]

Always speak clearly, calmly, and confidently. Always get your act together before you go on stage. And always use Script C.

ASK RIGHT, AND ASK THE RIGHT PERSON

You can do all the right things and still not get what you're asking for if you're not asking the right person. You have to know where the power is, who really has the decision-making ability, or your efforts will be in vain. Prior research will usually clue you in to who the right person is, though there'll be times when only trial and error will lead you to the decision maker.

Don't be irritated or complain when that happens. A lot of people have turf to protect or ego to inflate. Your job is to keep everybody on your side and let them help you find the person who can say, "I need you and I can buy."

Kay found this out when she was hunting for her very first job. A half-dozen times she went into offices and spoke with the receptionist or secretary. A half-dozen times she heard, "There aren't any jobs open in our sales department." When she began to hear about friends who were getting sales jobs at the same companies she'd called on, it dawned on her that the people she'd spoken to either were uninformed or didn't want another attractive female on the premises.

Kay learned fast that to get action, she had to go where the action is—to the sales director or president of the company and not to a person in a lower management position who couldn't say *Yes* or *No* if he or she wanted to.

NOW FOR THE FINALE ...

Now you know what you're after: which job, how much of a raise, what promotion. You've pinpointed the prospect you'll talk to. You've researched and have a bank of information. You've built a chain of contacts. So far, you've made all the right moves. You're almost ready for action. Read on.

THE IMPORTANCE OF DRESS REHEARSALS

My partners and I have the habit of always thinking, ahead of every meeting, "If we could write the script of what's going to happen—of what we *want* to happen and of what *can* happen—how would the script go?" Then we sit down and write it six ways to Sunday.

We decide what the goal of the meeting is: to get a definite *Yes* or *No* decision, or to get an appointment for another meeting. We work out all the possible variations and nuances that can make or break it for us. We try to think of every detail, so we won't find ourselves grappling with unpleasant surprises. This kind of preparation has become automatic with us. It's amazing how it's increased our effectiveness.

Successful people know exactly what they're going to do before they do it. Orchestra leaders follow scores, architects build according to blueprints, ballplayers have practice sessions, and people who sell well, sell according to a well-rehearsed plan. If you think rehearsing is a difficult and time-consuming exercise, think of it this way: With the same time and energy you'd spend complaining and worrying about the presentation you're going to make, you could educate yourself instead, and help guarantee profit and productivity.

Being prepared for what you want to make happen at a sales presentation is winning a major portion of the game before it begins. It arms you with confidence and lets you present yourself, or your product or service, in the best possible light. It puts you in command—of yourself, your fear, and the selling situation itself. Rehearsal is a power factor, one of the most effective tools you can use for success.

SETTING THE SCENE FOR REHEARSAL

An obvious parallel to rehearsing a sales presentation is rehearsing a play. The compositions are the same: Each has a cast of characters, costumes, setting, props, theme, acting style, dialogue, timing, and an audience. Think in terms of a theatrical production, then, and let's run through the elements of rehearsal for success.

The details of your production are important: how you look, where you are, what you say. But it's the sum of these parts that has impact on the effect of the production, not the pieces that go into it. The following are guidelines, because there is no single correct way of presenting yourself. You just have to be aware of what your details add up to.

If you're a person whose signature is wearing blue jeans and sandals, and it's important to you personally to wear them even at a presentation to an ultra-conservative prospect, you're entitled. That's you. Your costume isn't going to make or break the sale, but you are going to have to work harder to convince your prospect of your credibility, having foregone that particular item of support for your professionalism. If you're a helter-skelter type and it seems false to you to suddenly put your office in clinical order for the benefit of a certain prospect, so be it. You'll have to make up the lost points created by an untidy setting by being strong in other aspects of your presentation.

THE CASTING SESSION

The star is you. Or you and your team, if you work together with associates. The audience, your client or customer, is the partner you work with regularly, or a friend you can call on to help. It's very important to have someone else play opposite you, rather than trying to imagine the audience's reaction in your head. You need another person's mind and voice to respond to you, negatively and positively, to come up with arguments you might not think of yourself, and to provide analysis and suggestions.

Establish who each character is. The client or customer you'll be playing to may be conservative, hardnosed, easygoing, flip, mature, insecure, or any of the diverse personality types that abound. You're one up if you're already familiar with your prospect's personality or can find out what to be aware of—information that comes from people who've dealt with him or her.

If you're going to be facing an unknown quantity, do some digging so you'll be informed about the image of the company your prospect represents. Study the company's annual reports, and get all the background information on them by connecting to the many on-line business databases or web sites on the Internet (either by subscribing to a service that plugs into your home computer or using the facilities at the public library). You can call and ask the company's public relations department for copies of the principals' speeches and public statements, or even buy a share of stock so you'll have personal access to inside information.

By all means, use a credit rating organization and ask other suppliers, if possible, to find out if you're going to be romancing a person or firm that pays its bills, before you waste your time and energy making a pitch.

Whatever your prospect's type, you must know how to deal with him or her. With your buddy in the role of the prospect, you'll discover how to use your own style to advantage. You'll also become aware of how you appear to those you sell to. Francesca, a boutique owner, says that the process of stepping back and seeing herself as if she were on stage has helped her identify and then strengthen what it is about herself that customers respond to best:

> People pick up clues when you're not being direct with them or are devious in any way. I'm naturally a straightforward person and I try to project that directness in a casual way. I find that my style lets me establish rapport with customers without putting them off.

Chris is a state representative who's been elected to office three times. She says every election year is another sales campaign, and every address is a pitch. "My presentation style is to play the teacher. I think of myself as an expert in government administration, and I'm able to project that expertise so that people trust and believe in my authority."

Sally had to learn to temper her naturally easygoing style. She felt it inappropriate to her functions as director of a national fundraising organization. "In fact," she added:

> ... the way I come on when I'm not thinking about it would be out of place in many kinds of business situations. It implies a certain familiarity that should not be there. Especially if it's a first interview with somebody, I tone down my style at least until my professional credentials are well established. The rule of thumb I've developed is that assuming familiarity is never appropriate.

The creative director of a small advertising agency explains the effectiveness of team style, in which one member's personality balances and augments the others'. She told me:

> There are three of us who own our agency. Jackie's the president, Sue is the account manager, and I'm the creative director. When we're pitching a new client, Jackie will be the peacemaker—the arbitrator who jumps in with compromise solutions when Sue and I seem to disagree, and who makes the concessions that move stalled negotiations along. She comes off as the Scrooge who'll supervise every nickel and dime of the client's budget to make sure it's sensibly spent.

> Sue, the one who'll be working directly with the client, combines her professional understanding of advertising with a naturally cheerful personality. What clients get from her is a feeling of trust and friendship. They have faith in her business smarts and feel at ease with the nonintimidating way she gets them to do what's good for them.

> I get away with being a little over the edge, the "typical creative crazy" who's fun to be with because I'm different from the businesspeople they see every day. I can play the right amount of "attitude" they can count on to somehow produce the offbeat and consistently effective advertising that is our agency's hallmark.

With the three of us presenting ourselves as a unit, what the clients see is an agency they can profit from; a team that will give them the common sense, dependability, financial responsibility, camaraderie, hand-holding, and the terrific creative juice they need.

I'm not sure any of us could carry off a client pitch as well individually as we do when we act as a team.

PRESENTATION STYLE FROM A PROSPECT'S POINT OF VIEW

A corporate president told me of an experience he had not long ago, when he was interviewing a number of women for the position of executive assistant. He said:

> It was a parade of characters. First, I got "In Your Face" Ilene. I'd known Ilene years ago when she'd been a secretary in another department. Now she presumed upon that connection. Sailed into my office casually, as if we were buddies, and opened the meeting with reminiscences about the good old days. "Hey," she informed me, "am I perfect to be your assistant, or what!" This without even asking what the job was about.
>
> She was so busy being sure of herself, she didn't notice I was a possible *boss*. She misplaced the reason she was in my office. Not to socialize, but to get a job with me. Her style was on overkill and, needless to say, she killed her chances.
>
> After I'd laid out what the responsibilities would be to the next candidate, she responded with, "Why should I take this job?" I answered, "That's something I cannot answer." As far as I was concerned, the interview was over. This woman was daring me to hire her!
>
> Candidate number three was overly accommodating—the type I never hire. These women anticipate what they think you want to hear and volley their good intentions at you. I'll ask, say, "What about hours?" The answer I get is something like, "I never think about time when I love a job. If I have to work on holidays, that's okay. I'll be here as long as it takes me to do the job."

Excuse me? Even workaholics take Christmas off, even if they don't mind working late every other night; most people feel inconvenienced about coming in on Sundays, never mind holidays. These glib types oversell themselves in every way. I often find references on a resume that don't check out, exaggerations about what they've actually done.

The winning interview was with a woman I'd also met a few years ago when she worked for one of my account executives. That almost counted against her because I'd known Peggy as the "flake" who was smart and competent, but who needed to grow up. Flakiness is okay when you're having a drink after work, but I had my doubts about how she'd do in an office situation that meant serious responsibilities.

To my surprise, Peggy wore a suit to the interview, not her funky jeans. Her manner was reserved, but friendly. She handed me her resume, saying, "Maybe you don't know all the things I've done since I left here." Then she addressed what she knew I considered was the problem: "I have a feeling you think I'm someone who'd watch *Beavis and Butthead,* and quote from the show! I'm not that 'rad' kid anymore. I want you to know that when I have a job to do, I do it and never mind anything else."

That earnestness plus the good references that checked out on Peggy's resume convinced me she was the person to hire.

WARDROBING THE STAR

I used to dress badly, thinking, let people accept me as I am. I wore six earrings in each ear and a nose ring. And I wondered why I wasn't getting the promotions. What I had to learn was to present myself so my appearance wouldn't be the obstacle to my success. Basically, I had to grow up. Good grooming is not a political decision—it's smart money.

The first impression you make on a person is one that will persist in his or her image of you, so it certainly pays to rehearse your presentation costume right down to the briefcase or portfolio you'll carry. Packaging yourself right is as important in selling as packaging a cereal or a moisturizer: When people see something that appeals to them, they want it and will pay for it.

The way you dress should not only be in keeping with your own style—whether it's conservative, arty, chic, or elegant—it should be in keeping with your prospect's style of business and personal point of view. The clue to how to dress for a meeting is the same as for what you wear to a party or football game: Be appropriate.

Bobbie, a stockbroker who deals in corporate portfolios, says what she wears depends on the level of the person she's seeing. She said:

> If it's not a high-level executive, I don't overdo my look because it would threaten them. After all, selling is relating to people. For top-executive meetings, I pull out the good jewelry, the big designer suit and shoes, the expensive silk blouse. If I'm going to a conservative firm or to see somebody in a small town where conspicuous consumption is frowned upon, I'll leave off the jewelry and pare down to a goes-anywhere Liz Claiborne suit.
>
> The look is always elegant; it shows I'm a person who's arrived. Though I prefer suits, sometimes I'll wear a red silk dress that looks very professional, even though the color's hot. It depends on who I'm seeing and how I want to be seen. I always carry a good leather briefcase and purse, and keep everything in them well organized so I won't be caught fumbling among loose tissues or spare pantyhose in search of business cards or brochures.
>
> I even write down, in advance, what I'm going to wear and what things I'll take with me on an appointment, to be sure that what I want is in the closet and not at the cleaner's or shoemaker's.

To Bobbie, and many women like her, selling is always being what she represents, and always representing what it is she does and is. If she's selling professionalism and quality, she has to be those things. "I have to be a class act," she said.

Nearly all of the successful women you'll see carry a purse for their personal things and an attaché case, briefcase, or portfolio for their business papers and products. It's wise to invest in well-made bags and cases; in addition to representing you as a person of discernment, they will last and look good for years. Keep them polished and cared for at all times, ready to appear on stage in gleaming condition.

THE PROPS

Your props are the selling tools of your trade. Your business card, resume, portfolio, and other materials reflect what it is you do and your style of doing it. Rehearsing which props belong in a specific presentation gives you the advantage of having time to select or create the exact tools that will sell for you in that situation.

Here's a checklist that will help you review your props inventory:

BUSINESS CARDS. Your card, like your letterhead, is you when you're not around, and you should invest in professional and tasteful layout, typeface, and stock. Include your name, title, company address and telephone where you can be reached, your fax number, and, if you have one, your E-mail address, too. Keep a supply of business cards in your purse and briefcase at all times; you never know who you're going to meet, or when.

RESUME. Always carry at least three resumes, in case your prospect has a colleague who can use you or wants an extra copy for the files. Tailor your resume according to the situation. Several women I've worked with have as many as five standing versions of their resume, each geared to a different aspect of the field they're interested in. If their standing resume doesn't fit a new situation, they're ready to whip up additional versions that accent activities and accomplishments in that particular field, and that eliminate or abbreviate irrelevancies. Tailor your resume, but keep it honest. People really do check them out.

CREDENTIALS. A variety of materials fall under the heading of credentials. Select those that apply to you at this point, and add others if and when they become pertinent.

PORTFOLIO. Especially if you are in a creative field, the only way a prospect knows what you can do is to see what you have done. Collect tear sheets, reprints, and samples of everything you are proud of. Assemble them in an organized manner and showcase them in neat, manageable form. Rehearse what you will bring to each specific meeting, selecting what is relevant to your prospect's needs to prevent having to wade through reams of papers during the interview in an attempt to find the samples that will sell.

PUBLICITY AND LETTERS OF PRAISE. Be prepared to present evidence of the positive things other people have said of you, your product, and your work. As with a portfolio of samples, assemble your publicity credentials in an orderly, easy-to-view collection.

PROMOTIONAL BROCHURES AND STATISTICAL INFORMATION. In most cases these will be pieces you will leave behind, for review by your prospect after you have made your presentation. Know in advance what it is you'll want them to have in their keeping. In addition to well-written, well-designed brochures and statistical facts and figures, you may want to leave publicity reprints, letters of recommendation, samples of your product and, certainly, your business card.

VISUAL AIDS. Now with super high-tech graphics, photoshop, paintbrush, and other computer software programs—and printers capable of easily reproducing what you design on the PC screen—there's no reason why you can't print out any number of visual aids to help make your sale. If you don't have a PC with graphics capabilities, finding one is simple enough: There are thousands of copy shops and computer work rooms—some like Kinko's are even national chains—and they do have the equipment. You can rent a PC station and the software you need by the hour and have a techie on staff help you work up what you need.

If it's appropriate, use slides, charts, or film at a presentation, and be sure you're thoroughly familiar with the material and have practiced exactly how to show-and-tell your way through it. When using visual aids, brevity and simplicity work best; the purpose is to dramatize and clarify your key points, not to sidetrack your audience's attention or let anyone forget why you are there.

For most people, less is more. They don't want to swallow endless charts and numbers; they can only digest the essence. It's your job to distill the information for them before you present your material, and to be prepared to follow up with a summary of how you arrived at the data and how it relates to the points you are making. Spend the time and money to have your material professionally prepared; sloppy or childlike craftsmanship can only work against you.

If you're planning a slide show or film, check out in advance whether the room is equipped with working electrical outlets and whatever sound and lighting facilities you'll need. Be certain that your own or your rented equipment is in perfect condition and won't bomb out on you.

THE STAGE SET

There are four probable settings for your meeting:

- at your place;
- on your prospect's territory;
- on neutral ground;
- on the Internet.

If the show is to be at your place, give thought to the impression your decor and accessories will make. Are they reflective of your business and the image you want to convey? Is the space clean and orderly? Is the atmosphere hospitable, the seating and lighting comfortable, the appointments convenient? Are you prepared to serve coffee or a meal graciously and efficiently? Are you in command?

Renee, a gallery owner, often invites clients into her private office where she can sell them on her gallery artists. She orchestrates each meeting from beginning to end, starting with the selling environment itself. The walls of her office are hung with two or three paintings by artists she represents who are not in the gallery show that month.

The lighting is designed to flatter the art and at the same time to make clients comfortable. The background—walls, flooring, upholstery, and accessories—is done in warm but muted tones, to produce a quietly cheerful and positive mood.

Renee's office desk isn't a desk at all, but a simple, round turn-of-the-century American table with just a simple vase of fresh flowers on it. Like the rest of her office furniture, the table could be in somebody's living room—a gambit that enables clients to visualize the paintings as they would look in their homes. In a sideboard, ready for instant use, are an automatic coffee maker, sets of quality dishes—some fine china, some rustic pottery, her choice depending on the customer—as well as silverware, ivory linen napkins, and fresh croissants, delivered to her that day by her favorite bakery. The setting Renee has created is well thought out, tasteful, and effective. It deliberately sets a mood that makes people want to own what they see.

Most of all, this method of showing her "product" widens her market: Clients see the work of the artist being shown in the gallery space that month, as well as other artists whose work is in her office. For special buyers who she knows are collectors, an invitation into her private office is a perfect opportunity to provide a "sneak preview" of work from an upcoming show, and presell it.

You can't control your prospect's territory, just hope it's hospitable enough to make your pitch. But when you are in the position of choosing a neutral or public place for your meeting, you are only limited to what is available in the area. There are options, including restaurants, lounge areas of large, upscale hotels often attached to their main dining room, hospitality suites, and airport conference rooms.

Whatever city you're in, you'll find that public places differ in their amenities. Choose the best. Look for details such as a decor that enhances your image, soundproofing, privacy, good food and service, and any other facilities you may need, such as telephones. (If you carry a cellular phone, do not answer it if it rings and disturbs the meeting.)

Shop around and plan ahead. Go over every minute detail with the appropriate manager well in advance, and then take out extra insurance by checking every detail yourself just before it's time for your meeting.

If you're connecting through the Internet, you can obviously make your contacts, do your pitch, or agree to your million-dollar deal "anonymously"—your contact or client need not know you're working on ten cylinders wearing a four-year-old stretched out sweatsuit, your living room strewn with the newspapers your cat has shredded in a game of "tunnel."

DEVELOP A DIALOGUE

> Selling is a very tense situation for me. I'm always anxious, because it's a situation that involves making a positive presentation of myself and I feel very vulnerable. I'm more secure having some sort of formula to fall back on, something I'm familiar with.
>
> I find that if I go over what's going to happen beforehand, it's like having a road map to someplace I've already been and I can navigate the main routes and side streets and detours as they come up.

In addition to your physical presentation and that intangible, your style, it is essential that you rehearse what you want to say at your meeting, so you can put your points across with the proper impact. It is also essential that you think through and rehearse what you may *not* want to say: the responses you'll have to make to objections and reactions you wouldn't plan on in an ideal scenario. Expecting the unexpected is a major component of successful selling, and being fully prepared for disagreement is a winning strategic move.

The following chapter contains a sampling of possible scenarios played out and analyzed for you. I urge you to study the scripts, adapt them to fit your own business or profession, and play them out with a partner, to get into the swing of formulating your own.

With your buddy, go over the questions you will ask in order to get as much information as you can about your prospect's needs and situation before you start selling. Line up the high points of your product or service and strategize how best to present them. Have your partner talk back to you, so you can respond with appropriate dialogue. Have her play the devil's advocate and give you arguments and objections, then practice ways you can respond that will convince her to agree with you.

Try closing the deal. Try negotiating the terms of your sale. Try several different scripts, and after each run-through get feedback from your partner and analyze what has happened. What did you do well? Where did you go wrong? How could you improve your performance? Replay the scene with the suggested improvements and see how it goes. Go through each scenario from opening small talk to closing, then switch roles with your partner, so you can get inside your prospect's character and understand his or her reactions. Play the dialogue out fully, so you'll be comfortable as well as prepared.

This kind of rehearsal is called coaching by many people and, as on a good sports team, effective coaching leads to success.

Reality: *In selling, as on the stage, the better rehearsed, the more effective the performance.*

THE APPLAUSE YOU HEAR MAY BE YOUR OWN

Selling is its own reward. The joy of persuading people and the satisfaction of accomplishing what you set out to do cannot be matched. They can be augmented, however, by material rewards you give yourself; rewards that are incentives for completing what may be difficult for you, and that provide the recognition you need and deserve.

Preplan your reward. If it's a big sale you're after and you make it, give yourself a big present as a bonus. Redecorate a room, take a trip, buy a new coat. If your accomplishment is smaller—just setting up and getting through a presentation, for example—give yourself a smaller gift: a manicure, a taxi ride, a self-indulgent dinner. The point is to acknowledge that you've succeeded in completing a cycle, and to establish one more solid reason for setting and completing goals.

Reality: *You are the only headliner you have. Make the most of your chances.*

NETWORK MARKETING

I went to a network marketing meeting held in the small auditorium of a youth center and got converted. I started out small, investing $200 in the products, seeing how I could sell, figuring out how to talk to people. It took me a year before I recruited someone. After two years, I quit my job in desktop publishing and devoted myself to the business. I'd never do anything else.

I liked the company and liked the products but I just couldn't get the system down! The woman who recruited me said, "Ruth! You're perfect for us—no one's got better 'people' skills!" It didn't translate into money for me. Being a nice, accommodating person didn't mean I was good at pursuing sales and recruits. I was rotten at it! I learned after four months of a lot of rejection that selling was the main thing, not being a nice guy.

All work requires selling a product, a service, or your personal skills. If you work in network marketing and want to quit, you can take those skills and experiences you've learned from the business and apply them to most professions. You leave the business of network marketing with something! And so do you enter it with something—that is, similar knowledge and skills.

A BRIEF LOOK AT NETWORK MARKETING

You hear tales of millionaires who achieved their success by selling cosmetics, body care lotions, nutritional supplements, environmentally safe and pure soaps and other indoor or outdoor maintenance products, car oil, art frames, and whatever else—and who made their money through an industry called "network marketing." Such success stories often inspire others to equal heights, but most who are inspired do not climb as high. In fact, a majority drop out, quitting at their lowest point, discouraged. They are rather like Ruth, who tells her story in the second quote that opens this chapter.

WHAT EXACTLY IS NETWORK MARKETING?

*The Woman's **New** Selling Game* would not be complete without including this fascinating industry. It's where you may find the career satisfaction you seek outside the traditional work world. Once known as "multilevel marketing," network marketing is, simply, a business that allows its sales representatives to recruit other sales representatives and to earn commissions from a specific level of those recruits.

What interests me about the industry is that you learn the basis of sales, although they never call it *selling*. And, you don't need special training, inside connections, or a large investment to get started—what you need is drive (a bit of that "fire in the belly"), interest, enthusiasm, and a sincere respect for the product you are representing. Even more important is your willingness to learn the subtleties of the industry and how to sell and recruit—and *not* quit before you've mastered it.

It's a great way to earn a lot of money because of its structure, but it's also got a "rep." The industry has a murky side—the tales of pyramids, scam artists, and companies promising paradise quickly have been true in some cases. Even companies selling high-end products such as advanced nutritional supplement formulas fronted by top athletes and promising a huge profit margin to distributors (people like you) have collapsed because of poor management and poor funding, and some from basic corruption. The names of these companies are forgotten by all but the hapless networkers who bought in and lost money, time, effort and, often, the nerve to try again for entrepreneurial independence with a creditable company.

Herbalife, Mary Kay, Amway, Avon, Nu Skin, and Shaklee are a few of the highly reputable companies you hear about all the time. Nu Skin, in fact, is the only network marketing company with a top 5-A rating from Dun & Bradstreet.

I found a number of interesting parallels between network marketing and the selling experience in general for you to consider, most importantly that *you may transfer skills to and from network marketing*. Here's how:

CONTACTS AND NETWORKS. Your contacts (your network) can lead you to a career, an apartment, or a husband. If you are an entrepreneur, your contacts become a very valuable natural source.

There are times when you're only as good as your network, or my Rule of Three multiplied, if necessary. You want as many contacts as possible, people who will go out on a limb for you. The more people you know or know well enough to call, the more you can succeed. Here's an example:

If I'm doing a seminar and need a high-powered speaker from a certain industry, I'll call someone in my network who has a vast network herself and tell her what I'm interested in. She'll say, "Sure, one of my clients is ... who knows a perfect Ms. High-power very well."

This is not unlike the structure of network marketing. If you're selling cosmetics and want to put together a network party of six women to sell to and recruit, you'd know who among your friends, family, and business associates to call first—and who they might call. But you don't just want six women who'll buy a lipstick. You want at least one potential recruit, a woman who'll be interested in the big picture: a career.

Paulette, a top network marketer who has consistently earned over $250,000 a year for the last 12 years, says, "This is my business—I show up for it." To Paulette, "showing up" means she makes the most of every interaction with her recruits and every new contact, doing her best to sell them and recruit them. She has been known to recruit at an airport—a two-hour delay waiting for a plane got her talking to the woman seated next to her in the terminal, and she used the time productively. In terms of contacts and networks, you'll find that:

- After awhile, you have an instinct for who will remain your customers and who has that fire—or who you can recruit. In standard selling, you also know to "extend the sale" and get a buyer to buy more—and when to stop selling.

- Some people resist being recruited into network marketing and then circumstances change; they're ready to join. A similar experience is common in my life: I'll call on people who never give me business, but happily give me other numbers to call. Years later, I get a call from them: They're ready to hire me.

- You build up a favor bank both in network marketing and in any other profession. That is, your contact does you a favor and you do one for her. Sometimes you're doing all the favors for one person, but those banks of favors come back to you—if not from the person you've helped, then from other people. Even though you're not ultimately using every person for profitability, the favor bank becomes another version of a support group. Network marketers can always find a support group in their company.

What we can learn from network marketing and bring to retail sales is this very supportive, rather than competitive, community. It feels good to be part of a strong population of people you can call who will prop you up when your confidence is low or give you yet another contact when you're flying high.

Goal Setting.   The quality of your grapevine and contact base may be important in both standard selling situations and network marketing, but goal setting is right up there with it.

Network marketing entrepreneurs must examine their goals every day and meet them; the same is true for any of us, inside or outside the business. What is your focus? Where do you want to go with this career or business? Do you just want to earn your x number of dollars a month and wait for the raises, or do you want to be in charge of how much you make? Know your goals and how to map them out, approach them realistically, and actualize them.

Selling a Product or Service.   It goes without saying that you cannot sell a product successfully if you do not understand, like, or use it. We've all faced a sales situation in which the seller doesn't know what the thing is made of or why it's better than another like it in the competitor's line. Inertia and boredom are not selling tools. Know what the product is, have an affinity for it, use the product yourself, keep up with newer versions, and walk and talk them. Such connection to your product builds your network marketing business or your sales figures in another industry.

INTERACTIONS AND MEETINGS. Network marketing often forces you to manage a group of people who are all being shown your product and told how your business works. There's noise, people talking at the same time, everyone wanting special attention. And you are there with a purpose—to sell them.

Whether you're at a network party or a corporate meeting with a group of executives sitting around a table at a place of business, your intent is the same: to give your pitch, deal with distractions and noise, and *keep your eye on the ball.*

WHAT'S THE APPEAL OF NETWORK MARKETING AND HOW DOES IT WORK?

Most network marketers aspire to earning a few hundred to a few thousand dollars extra a month. *Extra* is the operative word; most people have a job when they sign up with a company, and devote an extra 5 to 20 hours a week of on-the-job training, learning the business. Most people quit their day jobs when they met a goal and are sure they will earn as much or more than the salary they'd previously been paid. Then they expand their commitment to succeed.

How do they succeed? The easiest way to describe network marketing is to set up general examples.

You don't only have to sell, say, $100 worth of products yourself to earn your commission of say, $18. Rather, you earn money above that by recruiting others to sell the product who recruit others to sell—or your "downline" organization. Here, generally, is what you could expect to see outlined as the compensation plan of a network marketing company. Terms and percentages will vary from company to company, but the principle will still apply.

You may earn your money four ways:

1. *By selling to a base of customers,* who may change from month to month, and hopefully will increase in number. Here you buy products at a wholesale price from the company and sell at the retail price. You earn your commissions, which are paid by the company. These are called *retail profits* (money earned from selling the product directly to customers). Before you sign up, be sure to check and see if the amount between wholesale and retail price is satisfactory and worth your while in time and effort.

2. *By selling products to distributors downline from you.* These are *wholesale profits.* Amway is one company whose compensation package relies on this plan. That is, when you recruit someone into the company, they can only order products for their customer base through you. You get your percentage of the profits, calculated by the company. Depending on the company, if you quit the business, your downline people will either deal directly with the company and place orders for products ... or not. Again, each company has its formula and procedures.

3. *By recruiting others into the company,* who have a base of customers and who will also recruit others who have a base of customers. These profits are generally called *overrides,* or a percentage of the wholesale profits paid to you from your "breakaway" people downline.

4. *By excelling in sales and recruiting,* earning recognition and bonuses from the company. The Mary Kay company is known for ego-boosting bonuses for top achievers, bestowing on their representatives cars, diamond-studded bumble bee pins (the bee is their symbol of success), gala crownings of "queens," and more.

Again, although there are many different plans and downline structures, here's how your independent business may look on paper, which helps you figure out where you're going and how much you may earn:

Let's say you are recruited into the theoretical Shiny Opp Company by Alice. You are now in business. So, here's ...

ALICE
You

According to the company plan, Alice will earn a specific percentage of all your sales to your customers and of the sales of your recruits. You are in her Level One. At Level One, the Shiny Opp Company compensates Alice at 13 percent of sales made by all her recruits.

Now you recruit Betty and Candy. Alice's structure looks like this:

ALICE	
You	(Alice's Level One)
Betty, Candy	(Your Level One, Alice's Level Two)

At Level Two, the Shiny Opp Company compensates Alice at nine percent of sales. But since Betty and Candy are your Level One, you earn 13 percent of their efforts. Then you recruit Dee, Evie, Franny, and Gigi. Your structure looks like this:

ALICE
You
Betty, Candy, Dee, Evie, Franny, Gigi

Evie, on your Level One, is very ambitious, knows a lot of people, and is willing to go the extra mile. She not only has a good base of retail customers after six months, but she also manages to recruit two women, Helen and Iris. Your structure now looks like this:

ALICE	
You	
Betty, Candy, Dee, Evie, Franny, Gigi	(Your Level One)
Helen, Iris	(Your Level Two, Alice's Level Three)

Alice is still benefiting from her and your downline recruits. The Shiny Opp company only allows Alice to profit three levels downline; some companies will go downline six levels, each level down paying a smaller percentage of the profits. This means that if you recruit Janice, Kathy, and Mattie about now, these new recruits are placed on your Level One line like this:

ALICE

You
Betty, Candy, Dee, Evie, Franny, Gigi,
Janice, Kathy, Mattie, Helen, Iris

This means that Alice will continue to get her percentages from any business your new recruits bring in. However, she does not profit below her Level Three (Helen, Iris) which is your Level Two.

When you recruited Helen, you knew she had the stuff—what the industry calls a "leader." She travels out of her state, meets with an old school friend, and manages to recruit her and her neighbor. They are Norma and Olivia. Now you've attained "breakaway" status. That is, you've broken away from Alice after she reached her three-level limit. Now you're at the same point. It looks like this:

YOU

Betty, Candy, Dee, Evie, Franny, Gigi,
Janice, Kathy, Mattie, Helen, Iris   (Your Level Two)
Norma, Olivia   (Your Level Three)

Of course, you can still keep recruiting, building depth on your first level—that is, the people you recruit directly. And if you are a good motivator, hopefully a few of your recruits on Levels Two and Three will also build depth, adding to your income.

Now you know why this method was once called multilevel marketing.

How to Choose the Right Multilevel Company for You

Since the economy is changing and a multiplicity of skills and flexibility will determine part of your financial fate, network marketing can fill this niche. How do you choose a company? Ask friends? Sample meetings at different companies? Read about who's doing what? Which company should you join? The answer depends on you: what kind of products you are interested in and which ones you can sell—and sell others on—with urgency and enthusiasm.

Let's go back to the Shiny Opp Company. You hear good things about it; you like the distributors you've met; the financial plan sounds good. Is it? Here's what you should check out before you sign up with Shiny Opp:

- Is this a company that's stable, with a history you can check on? If it's starting up, what does "getting in on the ground floor" really mean? Will you lose money on ordering inventory and recruiting materials? Will your customer base realistically buy the products?

- What products will you be selling and recruiting others to sell? Are you interested in them? Would you prefer a company that distributes or manufactures environmentally safe products? Or cosmetics? Interior decor? Clothes? Do you have an affinity for the product?

  I interviewed Janet, a woman who joined a network marketing company because she connected to its vitamin line, but she soon found that her customers and would-be recruits were interested in the facials and cosmetics. Janet's problem: She didn't know how to maintain enthusiasm or keep an ongoing pitch about what she called "the superficial stuff." She told me:

  > The facial pack was made from some volcanic material, plus other miracle herbal ingredients—and I could only seem to mention the great ingredients twice to a customer before feeling myself getting agitated. It softens your skin and you feel better—what more could I say? I don't wear a lot of makeup and get really bored talking about doing your face. It dawned on me, finally, that I should have joined a company that sold more practical items. I wasn't the glamour type.

- Who do you believe? If you go to these meetings and hear the pitch or a friend has gotten you hot for the company—stop! Do the research, talk to people who are still in this company and love it and people who *were* in it and left. Find out what bothered them. Was it their own lack of enthusiasm or time, or the manner in which the company operated, or inferior products?

- Does the company have a strong telecommunications system set up? Are they up to date with an 800 or 900 number? Does the company have a system that allows group broadcasts, and does it do satellite broadcasting for sales, prospecting, and training?

- Can they fill orders quickly, and *how* do they do it? Is there an automated delivery service? Can you order one product at a time, and is there an extra charge for singletons? Can you order 24 hours a day? Can customers pay by credit card and check? Does the company provide printouts or tracking reports that tell you your customer's buying schedule or preferences?

    One six-figure-a-year distributor told me that she loves training people, almost as much as recruiting them. She said,

    > I was helped, coached, motivated, pushed, encouraged, all of it. That coaching made a difference for me in how well I did. Now I want to do it for my recruits. I think of those coaching and motivation sessions as free lessons you could spend thousands of dollars on. Instead, here I am—someone dedicated to making your business work. This is what makes the network part of network marketing so important.

- How much support will the company give their new (and long-term) recruits and how well do they train you? Do they provide videos about the company and its products to help you better sell the product or recruit someone?

- How good is the compensation package? Have you compared it with at least three others? Avoid a company that asks you to "frontload"—that is, invest in a large inventory of products or "buy" recruiting kits.

WHEN OTHERS TELL YOU TO SAY NO TO NETWORK MARKETING

It's important to mention a common occurrence when you join (or think about joining) this business—the barrage of negative opinions about network marketing. Prepare to be discouraged, if not treated with scorn, by family, friends, and associates at your old day job.

The old tarnished image of the industry still influences how people view it, and they will be shocked that you're participating in it. Even if you convince them that signing up with, for example, Mary Kay Cosmetics simply makes you a beauty consultant with the intent to add to your self-esteem and your income (your truth) and not a schemer out to force moisturizer on poor single women raising three children alone (their exaggerated conception), some of them will still not be interested or convinced.

There are three standard reasons for discouraging you: Family and friends want to keep you as they know you and worry that you'll succeed, move away, and forget them. (Or, they fear that you *can* do it!) The second reason is that certain friends and family may cling to destructive patter that is meant to stick to you. It says you can't strike out on your own and make a lot of money, nor do you have a good "business head." (Or, they fear they'll lose their control over you. By telling you that you're weak, dumb at business, or a loser, they hope to keep you down!) The third reason—and this is credible—is that they worry you'll choose a fly-by-night company that will pull out of the business about six months to a year after a meteoric rise, and leave you down a few thousand dollars.

Global suggestions from people in network marketing who've heard every warning argument about entering the business are these: Don't argue with anyone more than once about what you can and cannot do and what you will or will not do in network marketing. The second time someone says, "I don't know why you're wasting your time on this and embarrassing me," just tell them calmly, "I'm in this business now. Sit down and I'll explain what it means to me and how it works, or let's move on to something else." Period. Don't waste energy or get suckered into time-wasting and soul-bending emotional scenes that go nowhere.

Of course, be sure that you choose the right company—one that's reliable, one with smart fiscal organization and planning, one you can deal with directly and take your suggestions and complaints to, and a company with a good product—one that is worth the effort you will put into it. Then if anyone says, "How low can you go?" ask them to sit down, try your product, and watch to see how high you can go.

PRO: WHAT NETWORK MARKETING CAN DO FOR YOU

On the far brighter (and more profitable) side of the picture, network marketing can grant you opportunities to gain personal confidence and financial independence in a way that a traditional job could never do. When you learn the skills to making network marketing work, you are an entrepreneur, not just a salesperson.

Every network marketing company is different in what they sell and what they call their representatives. Language changes from company to company; for example, they don't use the word "selling," and rarely tell you you're part of a salesforce. They call you a "distributor," a "representative," a "design consultant," a "beauty consultant," and so on, but never a salesperson. Whatever they call you, learn the business if this is your goal. When you master it, network marketing can offer you:

A SUSTAINING PARALLEL CAREER THAT PROVIDES EXTRA INCOME. This amount is determined solely by you and no one else. That is, keep your day job (or stay home to raise your children), but put in a certain number of hours a week to insure your financial goals. Which leads to ...

THE CHANCE TO MAKE THE KIND OF MONEY YOU DREAM ABOUT. Those dreams can mean you want an extra few hundred or few thousand a month to pay for necessities or incidentals, or you can make the career jump and set a goal to earn a six-figure income. Even if you don't reach star level and just earn that extra money, you're learning skills, and getting confidence.

THE ENCOURAGEMENT TO BE OPPORTUNITY-ORIENTED and to seize the opportunity the industry offers. If you choose the right company and the right associates, you will not be a lonely networker, left to tend to your own business at your kitchen table, unsure of how to proceed after a certain point. Instead, because of the structure of the industry, team support and motivation rallies enthusiasm and fosters skills. Opportunity can turn you into a successful entrepreneur.

INVALUABLE TRAINING.   If you are willing to be coached there will be people to help you. All of business today is the team experience. I asked the very dynamic Susie Greenwood how she handles training within her company, DDD Enterprises, a distributor of Nu Skin. She gave me an example of one woman who'd reached a crossroads where frustration seemed to run down two main avenues—she couldn't seem to increase either her sales or her recruiting. Susie told me:

> When you're in this business, one thing a leader doesn't do is bring our recruits business—*you* must focus on getting the customers. That's your inventory. And if you don't know people or have the ability to develop a big customer base, the business is impossible.
>
> I sat down with Ellie and we talked about her two big issues. I listened to what she'd been doing and what she thought was going wrong. Then I described how she could move the products better, and mostly, how she could use the little time she had harder and smarter. She wanted to be a leader, but the truth was, she didn't have time to move into a leadership position. Instead, we focused on what she could succeed at. I taught her to focus on where the money is and would be.
>
> I spoke to another woman in a similar position. Sharon had just moved to New York, and even though she wants to be a leader, right now it's impossible. She's working the dinner shift, waitressing—and that's not the problem. It's that she knows nearly no one in the city, hoping to break into what we call a cold market.
>
> Network marketing is a business for someone who is willing to meet a lot of people; someone who's entrepreneurial and a self-starter. If you want to succeed, be someone who can also motivate others to sell the business to others, and to keep them motivated.

Leaders can show you how to increase your business and ask for money. By modeling your actions on theirs, you will learn. Think about what your good role models tell you; notice how successful people get energy for the work and duplicate their actions for yourself.

When you're in this business, there are people like Susie Greenwood in every company—people who will advise you, help you break down your goal into manageable pieces, and help you see the bigger picture.

BUILDING A WIDE RANGE OF INTERPERSONAL SKILLS.   Nothing builds confidence like a good track record. Self-esteem, an old-fashioned idea, is one of the great byproducts of your success.

How do you get it? This is a business that asks you to develop a wide range of skills and helps you cope with rejection. This is important—you must accept rejection and go on with enthusiasm because 90 percent of the time you'll be rejected. If you're with a network marketing company, you are now an entrepreneur, managing your own business. Remember, every level you reach and build *is* your business—and to be successful, you need confidence and the ability to talk to people.

Many stand-up comics, when they start out on club dates, rig a tape recorder and tape the act. This is not to collect a record of the performance but, later, to critique the "set." They can hear where the laughs were and were not, whether the delivery was right for a joke, and if they sounded confident. Even comics with a whiny, self-effacing style on stage are still strong performers—you know they'd be fast and furious to defend themselves and their point of view. The message is: Even if the comic heard a lot of insults from the audience and one faint chuckle, she goes back on that stage the next week, making the changes in delivery, attitude, or whatever. The comics who get no laughs and don't get up in front of an audience again were never meant for comedy or for show business and should stay behind a desk. The comics who get up on stage and attack an audience who will not laugh at the same bad jokes should also keep their day jobs—they're not "leaders."

Do your own version of taping a stand-up act. You gain confidence as you enhance interpersonal skills and go through the process of selling and recruiting. Be hard on yourself at first as you analyze your meetings. Examine how you deliver your presentations. Remember what your potential recruit or customer said and how you countered. Did you "extend the sale" and keep her interested, or give up, show irritation, or become argumentative? What interested her most about the business or products?

Network marketing also forces you to break through the paralysis of facing the unknown—you learn how to speak to and capture an audience one-on-one or at a public meeting. You'll learn how to use your contacts, get your message across in terms of timing, and accept that it's okay to have setbacks as long you start again.

MAKING THE SALE NOW.   This is commonly overlooked, but much of making a sale (or signing up recruits) is sealed with a sense of immediacy! Network marketing helps you use that perception of urgency—your customer or would-be recruit is so charged up by your presentation, she's got to have the product or the business! Most people in sales don't create that heat anymore. Develop a style that says "take this now," and then expedite the product or service.

Leaders in network marketing can teach you to think about such speed, or, if you're turned down, to go on gracefully to the next person.

CON: THE DOWNSIDE TO NETWORK MARKETING

Multilevel marketing has been so scrutinized that we can look at it and say, "This is for me, and here's why," or, as one detractor told me, "I can think of at least two professions I will never enter—multilevel marketing and prison guard." The detailed analysis of this business helps steer you one way or the other.

Knowing the downside of the business is a way to arm yourself with important information, revealing the impossibilities. They are:

HARBORING OVERBLOWN FANTASIES ABOUT HOW MUCH YOU WILL EARN AND HOW FAST.   No other career path as easily seizes the imagination—perhaps other than show business, where dreams of sudden celebrity and riches command such fantasies of success. The magic of "making it big" is part of the sell. Before you sign up, keep the enthusiasm, but tone down the lofty dreams.

It's common in almost every network marketing business to go for the big pitch. Those standing at the front of the room talking to a group of recruits-to-be tell them, "Hey, stop what you're doing, join this company and make your fortune!" Recruits-to-be think they can make it in six months. *It won't happen.*

Susie Greenwood, the DDD distributor we mentioned earlier, is successful in the business, and her success places her in the industry's top percentage of big earners. Susie told me:

> A friend of mine came to a Nu Skin presentation and was excited by the numbers. Later she said, "Susie, this business is for me. But I only want to work five hours a week to make $700,000 a year." And she was serious! I told her to buy a lottery ticket.

I learned the business from a man who built a seven-figure income in 26 months. How did he do it? Hard work and some luck—he hit the company in a time of great momentum. I joined when there wasn't momentum, which made growth slower, but I loved what I was doing and where the company was going.

I've been building my business for two years—and I still often work a 20-hour day, weeks at a time, recruiting, teaching, motivating. Successful network marketing people know what it takes to make those numbers and how much time you really need.

As Susie points out, know that hard work is real but hype is smoke. Nu Skin is growing under what's called "infinite momentum," which means the company's still growing after it's matured. Amway, Mary Kay, and Avon are other companies that are still growing. Understand your goals and where you should place them.

BAD FIT—THE INDUSTRY IS NOT FOR YOU BUT YOU'VE MADE AN INVESTMENT IN IT.

Sheila, a teacher of desktop software at a computer school and an industry drop-out who lives in Connecticut, added her reservations about the business. Sheila dropped out of a company we'll call Bitter-Batter, Inc., which sold health supplements—products she believed in, but belief wasn't enough. "First," she told me, "there was the classic marketing plan emphasizing success in a short amount of time—big-time hype. And I bought it." Then she was advised to buy an inventory of products as well as a few recruiting kits, which cost her, all told, about $2,500.

Sheila was enthusiastic about the business, until two months passed. She discovered that she had no idea how to sell the company as well as her products. She hadn't brought in one recruit. *Remember, recruitment is the name of the game*—you earn more money when you can get a percentage of what your recruits earn. Plus, Sheila found herself abandoned by the woman who'd recruited her, a woman who'd promised to help, but said, "It's my policy not to be a mother and talk on the phone night and day. I know you can handle it."

Desperate, Sheila found others in the company who gave her tips on making some money and also attended Bitter-Batter meetings, but she learned too late that network marketing was not for her.

She said:

Most people come and hear impressive presentations—and the deal sounds good. But suddenly you're not focusing on what *your* goals are, you're being led down a path and meeting *their* goals and signing up. Then the business is not for you. I'd say, know who you are! I thought I'd be okay with the business, but it turned out I don't want to approach people and ask them to buy or join. That ends my career right there. Too bad I found out about this too late, after I'd invested a lot of time and money.

I spoke to a man who'd risen fairly high in the business who offered a few important caveats: He said to be aware of deceptive leaders who act like executive recruiters—people out to get people into the business, never mind the fit. He also told me:

If I have a criticism of this business that's been very, very good to me, it's that certain people with influence tend to exaggerate benefits, or simply set up a false representation in three areas. They are: what the product will and will not do; what income is expected for everyone; and what the business is about.

Always be aware that when you hear a leader say, 'we're looking for the right people,' *know yourself.* Not everyone *is* right—so know if you are."

Let's see exactly how all this occurs in the selling game—in action. The next chapter provides techniques you can use for retail sales, network marketing, or selling yourself, and you'll find out what's happening in the sale while it's happening.

THE ANATOMY OF A SALE

I think selling is really convincing people of the importance of what it is you're selling. It could be anything, even an abstract idea. First, you have to be knowledgeable and second, aware of the benefits of what you want to sell them.

Just as there are many types of sales, there are many variations in the selling process and no single script can apply to all the different situations you'll encounter. Keep in mind that what you're selling may not be unique, but a commodity that others may be pitching, too. How you sell it and who you know are the only real differences. The basics of the selling process are always the same. You open, you explore for information, you meet objections, you negotiate, and you close. One of these phases may be brief, another lengthy; each stage will vary with each sale. Their sequence may be shuffled around and some may not enter into certain pitches at all.

What follows is an overview of the facts of making presentations: the anatomy of selling. The scenes and commentary here are guidelines, since there's no across-the-board formula for making a sale. I'll explore and analyze the dynamics of several different situations in this chapter. You can adapt the theories and techniques to various selling situations by shifting the elements of timing, sequence, emphasis, and style as needs dictate.

SCENARIO I. THE ANATOMY OF A SALE FROM OPENING TO CLOSING

CAST.   Jenny Hanson. Account executive for a New York public relations agency. Her goal: to sell a new and sophisticated financial marketing concept to a Midwestern corporation. She is wearing a fashionably tailored suit and blouse. The look is professional and business-oriented; Jenny is there to make a sale, not to socialize.

PROSPECT.   Senior management team of Fortune 500 company. President: warm, pleasant; wears $850 Brooks Brothers suit. V.P./Finance: pleasant but distant; dressed in brown plaid suit with vest. Public relations director: suave, charming, tries to put everyone at ease.

SETTING.   The president's office: Persian rugs, brown leather sofa, mahogany bookcases. Office and executives' clothing say "very conservative, very masculine."

JENNY: [*Just before meeting, she yawns deeply and says to herself:*]

Be organized. Compose yourself. This is good for them. You are going to aid them, so you shouldn't be concerned. You are offering a service that's going to be marvelous, to sell a concept for them, so it's to their benefit that you are here.	*Yawning* relaxes her tense muscles, giving herself a pep talk reduces tension about going into a situation that is new to the prospect.

JENNY: I'm pleased to meet you. I'm Jenny Hanson. Thank you for the coffee.

PRESIDENT: Did you have a good flight in?

JENNY: Very pleasant and right on time. And it's such a nice day! Well, actually, it isn't. It seems to me it's always cold when I'm in Chicago. Do you ever have good weather?	*Opening* small talk. Friendly. Nonsubjective. Topics they can all agree on. Relaxes tensions, establishes human connection.

V.P.:   (*Laughter.*) We do have good weather from time to time.

JENNY: I think it would be of great assistance, as I mentioned to Jim, your PR director, and of great importance for your company to participate in this year's International Investors'	*Makes transition* from small talk quickly, once tensions are relaxed. *Pitch* states why she is there; points out features of

Conference. This is our second conference and we had a great number of Europeans express interest in your company last year at our West Coast meetings. As I mentioned in my letter to you, we are expecting between forty and fifty European institutional investors this year, basically the portfolio managers and decision makers.

what she is selling; opens discussion to questions and objections that will tell Jenny more about company's areas of need.

PRESIDENT: Why do you think that's going to be of assistance to us?

Interest aroused; wants to know more.

JENNY: You have a great deal of outstanding stock, Europeans are very interested in your company, and this is an excellent opportunity to put those two facts together.

Immediately answers with *benefit* to company. Shows she has done *research* and knows her business.

V.P.: Why isn't it better for us to go to Europe on our own than to meet with a group of Europeans here?

Mild *objection.*

JENNY: First, by going to Europe, you'll be taking manpower away from your office. The three of you, as the senior management team, would have to go. Second, you can only hit ten institutions at the most in a week's time, if you keep really busy. And they're not all going to be able to see you. By attending the conference instead, in the space of an hour and a half you can speak before forty to fifty key investors who represent nine different countries. You couldn't possibly do that in a week in Europe, could you?

She has thought through this objection and her answer beforehand, during *rehearsal.*

Blends objection with strong *benefit.*

Poses question that will get *agreement.*

PRESIDENT: You're right. You have a very fine concept. But I would feel

Gets *agreement.*

	awkward paying a PR firm $4,000 for one and a half hours of these Europeans' time. It's as if I'm buying their attention.	*Objection* to cost.
		Shows conservatism.
JENNY:	Quite the contrary. You and four other companies will be paying the Europeans' expenses with that $4,000. And that cost includes the fee for our public relations firm.	*Handles objection* by justifying and diminishing cost.
PRESIDENT:	I see. That sounds like a good idea.	*Agreement.*
JENNY:	Yes, I think this would be extremely worthwhile for you. You know, the $4,000 for the hour and a half with your key prospects is the same as three tickets to Europe that would take your key people out of the office for a week.	*Supports agreement* and reinforces *benefit* of cost efficiency.
V.P.:	I must say I'm somewhat leery. You've only held one of these conferences before. Are these the decision makers who attend? What other companies have signed up on this?	*Objection* shows he needs credentials and endorsement.
JENNY:	The ABC and XYZ companies have both signed up. They're both Fortune 500 companies, also, as you know. There are others, but it's premature to mention them. But you are in good company, I assure you. Here is the list of corporations that participated last year, major corporations and financial institutions. They found it a very successful venture. I'll leave these brochures and letters with you, if I may.	*Supports* need by providing *validation.*
		Came *prepared* with documentary *validation, proof* of performance, *leave-behind* pieces.

V.P.:	I do think it's a good idea, and we would like to consider participating. Could you tell us a bit more about your firm?	*Agreement* and *interest.* Still needs *validation.*
JENNY:	Here is some literature you may keep. It has a list of our clients, tells what we do for them, and there are some reprints of news items on us as well. Now, it's fortunate that I'm here at this time because we still have one of the first-of-the-week slots open for your presentation, and it would be to your advantage to choose an afternoon slot starting at four o'clock so you could move right into a reception and dinner that you can sponsor. That way you'll get extra time to talk with the European investors.	*Came prepared* to document her firm's credentials with leave-behind pieces. Having heard *interest,* moves immediately into *trial close.* Takes risk of losing the sale by *limiting choice* to time company may not be able to use. *Extends* sale by adding *benefit* of sponsoring meals PR firm would otherwise have to pay for.
PRESIDENT:	That's a very good idea. What kind of money would that run into?	
JENNY:	That would be perhaps $1,500 at the most. However, with that additional time, you can get into social conversation and create personal rapport, which you can't really do in the hour and a half you'll be speaking from the podium.	*Justifies* cost by turning it into a strong *benefit.*
V.P.:	Your propositions sound very good. We want to think about it.	*"Maybe."*
JENNY:	Fine. Why don't I give you a call this Friday for your answer? Meanwhile, if any questions come up, please call me. Thank you very much for taking time out of your day to see me. I appreciate it very much.	Puts a *time limit on Maybe* and *asks for decision,* while allowing time for company to check on PR firm's credentials. *Ends meeting,* knowing *strong interest* has been expressed.

Follow-up. Jenny keeps in touch during the interim by sending individual thank-you letters to the three principals, restating her proposition and the benefits she can provide for them:

"I thoroughly enjoyed meeting with you last week regarding the International Investors' Conference. I do hope you and your associates will be able to make the presentation of your company's background and growth potential. I know from our surveys that Europeans are interested in your company. At this time we have tentatively slotted you into Thursday, November 4 at 4 P.M., and I will be in touch with your office to discuss the logistics of your presentation.	Restates *purpose.* *Adds* idea. *Supports* benefit. *Assumes Yes* decision.

     Thank you again.
     Cordially, Jenny Hanson"

Closing. Jenny relates how she closed the sale:

Forty-eight hours later, I called the president. I prefer going to the top because that's where the ultimate decision is made, and I would much rather try to talk him out of a *No* than talk other people into rediscussing it with him. He said, "We'd like very much to participate. Please be in touch with our vice president of finance, who will be handling all the arrangements."

We wrote a contract on our firm's letterhead stating that the company had agreed to make a presentation on November 4 at four o'clock at a fee of $4,000, half of which would be paid sixty days prior to the conference, with the balance coming due thirty days after the conference. The contract also stated that the company would sponsor a reception and dinner, and that my PR firm would be available to assist them in all the logistics. It was a win–win sale.

SCENARIO II. (The following illustrates one of the many possible variations on this sales presentation. The cast, setting, and situation are the same as in Scenario I.)

JENNY:	I'm pleased to meet you. I'm Jenny Hanson. Thank you for the coffee.

PRESIDENT:	Did you have a good flight in?	
JENNY:	Very pleasant and right on time. And it's such a nice day. Well, actually, it isn't, is it? It seems to me it's always cold when I'm in Chicago. Do you ever have good weather?	*Opening* small talk. Friendly. Nonsubjective. Topics they can all agree on. Relaxes tensions, establishes human connection.
V.P.:	(*Laughter.*) We do have good weather from time to time.	
JENNY:	I think it would be of great assistance, as I mentioned to Jim, your PR director, and of great importance for your company to participate in this year's International Investors' Conference. This is our second conference and we had a great number of Europeans express interest in your company last year at our West Coast meetings. As I mentioned in my letter to you, we are expecting between forty and fifty European institutional investors this year, basically the portfolio managers and decision makers.	Makes *transition* from small talk quickly, once tensions are relaxed. *Pitch* states why she is there; points out features of what she's selling; opens discussion to questions and objections that will tell Jenny more about the company's area of need.
PRESIDENT:	We're not even in *The Wall Street Journal*'s stock exchange listings, so why do you think this will be of importance to us?	*Objection* that provides *information.*
JENNY:	I beg to differ with you. You are most definitely included in the New York Stock Exchange listing that appears in the eastern edition of the Journal. If you'll excuse me a moment, I'll call my office and we can check it out right away ... Yes, here are the quotations on your stock at yesterday's closing.	*Makes client wrong.* She could have said, "Of course, not living in the East you don't get a chance to see that edition of the *Journal.*" Points out that she did not offer an incorrect fact.

PRESIDENT:	Isn't that interesting. Do all our releases to Dow Jones go into *The Wall Street Journal*?	*Informs* her that President is inexperienced in area of public relations.
JENNY:	Well, of course they pick up all your dividend releases. If it's a story about new appointments in senior management, sometimes it'll be picked up and sometimes not. It depends on whether your story is as important to the writer as some other story that's breaking.	Provides helpful information but fails to *control agenda* and stay on *goal*.
PR DIR.:	As a matter of fact, she's right, Mr. Jones. That's the way it operates.	
JENNY:	Oh yes, these are the kind of things we do for our clients all the time: placing articles in *The Wall Street Journal*. Are you expecting a management change soon?	*Strays* further from *agenda* and begins to sell PR instead of investor's conference.
PRESIDENT:	No. Of course, that would be very hush-hush information, anyway.	Does not express *confidence* in Jenny.
JENNY:	Our main job is investor relations and we specialize in placing stories and interviews with financial publications to improve the image of our client companies or to make stockholders or potential investors interested in purchasing stock.	Has lost the *agenda*.
PRESIDENT:	That's very interesting. I didn't realize there are companies that specialize in that.	
JENNY:	Yes, sir. We represent a number of major corporations for just that purpose. Here is a list of our clients. But that's why I'm here today, to discuss your corporation and the European interest in it.	Tries to return to her *purpose* and revive interest in proposal.

PRESIDENT:	We aren't too eager to have our stock going out to Europeans.	*Objection* that opens opportunity to *explore* for information.
JENNY:	Can you tell me why?	*Asks* for *information.*
PRESIDENT:	Well, we're a Midwestern company and we like to have Midwesterners owning our stock.	Conservative. Jenny is in the wrong place. She should have determined *attitude* and *interest* before making call. She wasted her time by failing to do *research,* which would have told her that this company will require two to three years' *education* before she can sell an innovative concept to them.
PRESIDENT:	You do have an interesting idea, though. May I have your card, and we'll be in touch with you.	*"Maybe."* Very disinterested. Jenny will have to initiate any further contact.
JENNY:	Just a minute. It must be in here someplace. I'll find it.	Loses *control* by being disorganized and loses image of professionalism.

OPENING A MEETING

The technique of *opening* a meeting is fairly simple: Use small talk to establish rapport based on honesty that opens the lines of communication and begins to build agreement. Use a base of reality. Start by finding something in the office you truly admire, something that will put you and your prospect in accord. For example: "What a great view from your office. I love how the hills look so near the center of town, don't you?" (The reaction: Of course I do or I wouldn't have moved into this office and wouldn't keep my blinds up, no matter the season. I'm proud of it, too. She's nice to notice; we share the same sensibilities.)

Or, "Your collection of books on horticulture is impressive. Are you a gardener?" Now you can talk about your prospect's pet interest. Or, "What a lovely-looking child in this snapshot. How old is she?" Here you've opened up communications on an observation that strikes you, therefore, your comment is absolutely genuine for you. You've begun on an honest note that sets the tone for credibility and commonality as you go along. Later, as instinct directs, you'll be able to bolster that rapport with other truly-felt compliments on the person's actions as well as possessions. You might say, for example, "I admire your enthusiasm." Or, "You're so clear on your needs." The implication is that the two of you agree on style, taste, behavior, and probably the product or service you offer, too.

In your opening, as in every other communication you ever have with a prospect, always remember this inflexible rule: *Never make the other person wrong.* Your aim is to get agreement, not argument; to do business, not battle. The minute you make a prospect feel stupid, insulted, or inadequate, he or she is going to turn negative. There are simple and effective techniques by which you can acknowledge a person's error or difference of opinion without making him or her wrong. Phrases that turn the trick are:

- *That's a good point.* Let me add that in my experience, many people have quite different reactions to our product.

- *I can see why that's an important thing for you to know.* Our deliveries are sometimes slow, and I'd like to explain how the system works.

- *Many people feel as you do initially,* but after using our services they usually feel quite the opposite.

- *It's interesting that you bring that up.* I felt the same way at first, until my company ran a survey with results that surprised us all.

MAKING TIMING WORK FOR YOU

Your opening may be brief, as Jenny's was, or it may go on for five minutes or so if instinct tells you that your prospect is a chatty type and there's time for the amenities. Either way, be sure that *you* control the agenda.

There is something else to bear in mind about timing: It varies from region to region. In New York and other large urban centers, you're going to be given almost no time whatsoever for your entire presentation, from open to close. In other parts of the country, the pace is a bit more leisurely, but even they're moving more quickly to the agenda. A New Yorker's three minutes becomes ten minutes in other parts of the country. Take advantage of the time.

You'll want to match the prevailing tempo and corporate culture so you fit in, but you'll also need to protect yourself. Warming up your prospects in a leisurely manner may be a pleasant way to do business, but it can be costly when your time is money and you're geared to a fast track.

The best advice to nudge a meeting along is: *handle with care.* Move the conversation gracefully where you want it to go, in a way that doesn't display impatience or make the other person feel he or she is wrong. On the other hand, if you find yourself being rushed into a supersonic New York orbit, don't despair or feel insulted. You can still make all the points you've rehearsed clearly and effectively, minus trimmings.

CREATING THE RIGHT MOOD

Your style should set a mood of confidence. Make direct eye contact with the person you're addressing. Don't stare him or her down or avoid eye contact, but look directly at the person to whom you're talking; nobody wants to do business with a confrontational or shifty-eyed salesperson. Keep your body relaxed and open, and avoid nervous body language—smoothing your hair back in big dramatic gestures (like comics Dennis Miller or Richard Lewis), picking at your cuticles, taking your glasses on and off, chewing your bottom lip, or any tics or jerky movements that distract attention from your message.

Set the tone for your meeting by being enthusiastic. You needn't "morph" into an effervescent cheerleader, but show an enthusiasm that's in keeping with your natural style, bespeaks your positive outlook, and says, "I feel good about being here." Check your own ego at the door and let the other person do the talking if he or she is a talker. Support everything he or she says; don't try to one-up or make the other person feel stupid or ill-informed.

Observe the courtesies of introductions and name usage. In the same way that young children can't be sure which fork to use at their first formal dinner parties, office etiquette can bewilder women who are unaccustomed to business situations. The opening conventions are these:

- Introduce yourself to the receptionist (if there is one) or pick up the phone in the reception area and call the prospect's extension to announce that you're there. Introduce yourself to the people with whom you're meeting by giving both your first and your last names: "I'm Jenny Hanson." Add your company affiliation and position if the information is relevant or necessary.

- Unless you are asked to do otherwise, address people older than you by their surnames: Mr. Jones; Miss, Mrs., or Ms. Smith. When in doubt as to title, ask the secretary how your prospect likes to be addressed.

- Be alert to the conventions in generally informal companies such as advertising agencies and publishing houses, where the use of first names is usually preferred.

- Shake hands with everyone on entering and on leaving a meeting. Initiate the action yourself. It shows that you're an assured, professional woman.

- Give your business card to each person at the meeting, at the outset or as you leave, depending on the situation.

- Be generous with your thank-you's, and be sure to include recognition of the assistant who serves you coffee or provides other amenities.

Maintain an atmosphere that is courteous and friendly, but be certain you stay in control of the agenda so that you can get your message heard. Remember that whoever holds the agenda is in the seat of power, because that is the person who can include or exclude topics from the conversation. If things begin to get out of hand, as they are apt to do, you can stay in control by using the technique of the Three A's. They are:.

ACKNOWLEDGMENT, AGREEMENT, AND AGENDA-CONTROL

Here is a common situation from which the Three A's can rescue you. You are sitting in your prospect's office and he or she is distracted. There's a look of boredom, or impatience, or of being mentally out to lunch. The phone rings ceaselessly, secretaries run in and out, and your prospect is paying little attention to you. Instead of feeling you're intrusive or that you've invited disapproval, launch into the Three A's.

Start by *acknowledging* what's happening. Say, "You seem to be having an extremely busy day." Then get *agreement*: "I'm sure you'd like to complete what's going on in your office." Having given your prospect the opportunity to complete his or her cycle, go on to regain control of the *agenda*: "I'd like to present my story so you can understand it completely. It'll take ten minutes to tell you what I have for you. Would you like to take that ten minutes now, or would you rather complete what you're doing? I could wait outside for a few minutes and come back when you're done." Then, when your prospect has chosen between the two reasonable and considerate options you've presented, you can go on with your message, sticking to the ten-minute limit you promised and staying in control of the agenda.

MOVING INTO THE SALES PITCH

Make the transition from opening to pitch as soon as you feel that rapport has been established and tensions are relaxed. You may say something as simple as, "Let's get to the business at hand" or "Let me tell you why I'm here" to move the discussion forward. Or you might make the transition by using a piece of information you have that relates to the client's or customer's affairs and eases you into business talk: "I've been reading in the papers about the difficulties your industry has been having with strikes. I ran into our mutual friend, John Jones, yesterday, and he says you've had to cut back on production this quarter because of it." In this example, using a mutual contact's name adds further to your credibility.

The sales pitch usually begins with your stating or restating the reason for your meeting, and succinctly stresses benefits to your prospect. Beginners are apt to throw all 52 of their cards on the table at this point, a sure way of confusing a customer—and making no sales point at all. You should start by playing only your ace instead, describing the one major benefit your product or service offers to your prospect, the one card that will capture his or her interest.

For example, suppose you're meeting with a candy manufacturer. From research you've gleaned from newspaper items or inside gossip, you know that your prospect's major problem is the increasing cost of ingredients. Selecting the part of your company's service that fits into the problem, you lead off with the benefit you can provide: "I'm aware that you are having a great deal of trouble because of costs, Ms. Sweet. Our company has devised a process by which you can test whether using less sugar in your candies will produce a candy with customer appeal. Let me add that the idea of a candy with low sugar content will give you a big promotional advantage: Your ads can stress the healthier, low-calorie approach without loss of flavor."

Having captured your prospect's interest with something that will benefit her, you can then move into a brief visual or oral presentation that explains the features of the benefit. This should take no more than three or four minutes, at which time you can move into exploring for information about your prospect's needs, if you are not already fully informed.

EXPLORING FOR INFORMATION

When you know what information you want from your prospect, your exploratory dialogue will come easier to you. You know this pond has that fish. Sometimes you're not sure if the pond's got better and different fish downstream, and suspect they do. Other times, you don't know what you're missing! Don't worry about it. In either case, you'll still get the information you need and make the points you want to make if you are well prepared.

Your aim in *exploring* is to discover what the other person needs so you can offer to help (or, the fish you know about and the fish you didn't know about). You should come to each meeting with a prepared list of questions to ask, just as a reporter gets information with the Who-What-Where-When-Why formula. Here is a generalized list of questions you might ask:

- What are you doing now?
- How would you like to change?
- When would it be possible to change?
- Under what circumstances would you consider changing?
- What other considerations would you have?

More specifically, the situation might call for questions such as: What is the average salary of your employees? What is the average turnover per year? What is your peak production season? In which month do you ship? In which period are your profits lowest? When you have completed your questioning, you will have heard the answers from the other person. You won't be rushing to assumptions and he or she will have to stand on or expand on what's been said.

EXPLORING FOR CLARIFICATION

Listen *to* the lines and listen *between* the lines: Hear the answers to your questions, and what the other person is trying to say and is really saying. Play back the responses to be sure you understand each point clearly, and to extract more information. One effective way of doing this is to repeat the last words you hear as a question. It's what psychiatrists do all the time—at $150 an hour.

For example, the client says, "We have a shipping room situation that demands continuous rescheduling," and you respond with, "Your shipping room demands continuous rescheduling?" The reply to that will probably supply information, such as, "That's right. You see, orders for our goods come in lots that are sometimes large, sometimes small. What we need is a system that helps us keep track of the work flow so we're not wasting downtime."

Then you could move in with a direct offer: "So your concern is about wasting downtime? I see. I could set up a series of interviews with your people and analyze just how the waste can be cut and absorbed profitably, then recommend to you certain charts that would let you track your scheduling consistently."

Here is a sample exploratory script, complete with played-back questions:

Q: Why do you prefer brand *X*?

A: Habit, I guess. We always had brand *X* at home when I was a child, so I just continue to use it.

Q: Habit?

A: Well, I did try other brands, but I always came back to brand *X*.

Q: I see. You've tried other brands?

A: Yes, but they always seemed to lack that special something that brand *X* has.

Q: Tell me more.

A: Well, for one thing, brand *X* has just the right amount of sugar in it. It has a flavor the whole family likes. We never had a competing brand that everyone wanted to eat. I might like the sweetness of another one better, and the kids wouldn't. So I figured, why hassle the family? If everyone is going to eat *X*, why keep trying others out on them? Especially since the others are more expensive.

Q: More expensive?

A: At least a nickel a package more.

Q: Do you have any other reasons for preferring brand *X*?

A: No. Just habit.

Other exploring phrases to use are: Can you explain more? What else? In what way? I'm not sure I understand, tell me more. I see, and then what?

You can also get information from specific questions such as these: Do you have something particular in mind? What kinds of clothes do you feel most comfortable in? That color blue is flattering on you. Are most of your clothes in that shade? What would be your favorite outfit—one that you bought in the last two years? What was so right about it for you?

HIGHLIGHTS OF EXPLORING

Whether you are selling a product, a service, or yourself, the process is the same:

- Pinpoint your client's important needs by asking questions.
- Sell to those needs by presenting benefits.
- Assume nothing.
- Stick to your agenda.
- Inspire confidence.
- Get agreement all along the way.
- Summarize each segment as you go along.
- Say what you have to say pleasantly and with conviction.

GETTING INFORMATION FROM SOMEONE WHO WON'T TALK

Sometimes you meet a prospect who just won't respond to your probing. One way to get the information you need is to limit the questions to those requiring a *Yes* or *No* answer, such as: Are you looking for a loose or form-fitting dress? Do you like brand *X* better than the other brands? Is scheduling shipments a problem? Do you like natural wheat or rice cereals?

EXPLORING TO FIND THE HOT BUTTON

In the process of drawing out problems, you're going to find out what your prospect's greatest need is, the biggest desire, her hot button. Whether it's price, status, practicality, or something else, you want to hit that hot button, sell to your prospect's need, fulfill her desire by offering a benefit. In the following example, validation is added to the benefit of cost savings: "I can see what your problem is and why you're wary about investing in any more equipment at this time. You know, the ABC Company had a problem very similar to yours. They tried our system and it not only straightened out the problem, but ABC found its profits rose by 12 percent in the first year. And the investment in our equipment had paid for itself within the first six months."

Reality: *Ask and you shall receive. Explore and you shall find.*

THE TRIAL CLOSE: THE BIGGEST EXPLORATION OF ALL

As early as possible during your exploratory phase, the minute you get agreement on the points you have presented and your prospect shows interest, test the waters to find out whether the person you are speaking with actually has the authority to finalize the sale. This is the *trial close,* and it is the ultimate probe. What you are doing is finding out if you are in the right place and whether you should continue with your presentation or move on to somebody else. Clarifying your position through a trial close can save you an enormous amount of time, even though it is a risk that many people back away from taking.

A trial close can reveal vital information for you to work with. For example, early in your exploration, you might say, "Mr. Richards, it sounds as if you think these books are just right for your curriculum. I believe an order of 250 copies would be just right." Then, if your prospect counters with something like, "Two hundred and fifty books! What are you talking about? Fifty is as many as we can possibly use," you have received information as to what's considered a reasonable quantity. You've also confirmed that your prospect is definitely interested in your books.

You test the waters with, "Bob, a $100,000 contract with us sounds like what your company needs," and you get back this valuable information: "A hundred thousand dollars! That's madness; the most we ever spend is $10,000." Now you know what ballpark you're playing in.

You trial-close by asking for your prospect's signature on a contract and you hear, "Sign the contract! I'm in no position to sign contracts around here. You'll have to go to management with that." Wonderful! You've learned where the power really is. Go back and explore what slant the two of you should take for a meeting with the decision makers.

Reality: *It's scary to take risks; you have a chance of losing—you also have a chance of winning.*

HANDLING OBJECTIONS

Everybody is not going to agree with everything you propose. But disagreement or objection doesn't necessarily mean you've lost a sale. It means the other person has been listening to you, and that's a positive sign; it's an opportunity to go ahead and find out how you can win the sale.

Bear in mind that there are two kinds of objections: real ones and those based on personal opinion. Real objections are based on fact, such as, "Your prices are not competitive," "You lack experience, so I can't use you," or "We've had real problems with deliveries by your company."

A real objection requires an immediate answer or your sale will be stopped in its tracks. Most often it will be an objection you've heard before and anticipate hearing again, so you will have come to a meeting armed with refutation: documents, letters of recommendation, ad reprints. Then, when the objection arises, you'll be prepared with an answer: "Yes, you've made a really good point. Another of our clients had the same problem and we solved it very well. Let me show you the letter she sent me afterward." Or, "Yes, I've heard that before. Another client had the same initial impression you've just stated. He decided, even though he objected to the same point, to try our services on a trial basis. Here's a letter he wrote afterward telling how pleased he was. What had seemed like a problem to him turned out to be a very positive feature, as you can see by what he said."

Another good way to overcome a real objection immediately so as not to lose the sale is to take immediate action, such as calling your office on the spot and making an arrangement that will satisfy your client or customer. "You're quite right; our shipments to you last season were not on schedule. If I may use your phone, I'll call our warehouse manager right away and ask her to set up priority shipping for you."

A real objection has the further advantage of identifying a problem for you, thus enabling you to come up with the solution. Perhaps the objection is to price. You can shift the focus by slicing your cost into digestible portions. Let's say you're selling a service

that costs $500 and the customer says, "That's way too much money; I'm just a small business." You can make the $500 easier to cope with by dividing it into realistic bits: "Yes, and $500 for a whole year comes to less than $10 a week. That's not very much money for the service you'll be getting."

The second kind of objection, that based on personal opinion, deserves short shrift. Minimize it and get on to what's really important in your presentation. Off-the-wall objections can't be answered by documentation, and they're not substantive enough to stop your sale, so play them down. You can get past objections such as "I don't like red and I wouldn't have it in my store," and on with the flow of your presentation quite easily with answers such as "Yes, we all have personal preferences. I don't like red either." Or, "I'll be covering that point in just a few minutes."

For every negative or iffy reply, you'll find there's a question you can ask that will reveal areas of need not yet uncovered, needs that you may be able to fill. Begin by playing back each objection so you'll find the need, as in these examples:

Q: You say your budget is too tight at this time? Is that your main objection or is there something else that bothers you?

You're looking for another problem, one that you can help with.

Q: If I understand you correctly, you already have a data system. Does it include a memory capability?

You're finding a benefit your competitor cannot offer.

Q: I know how you feel when you say you don't really want this system because it would add procedural steps and be bothersome. Actually, my company will work out all the preliminaries and take care of the execution of them as well. So you see, your people won't have to become involved.

You're getting rid of that objection and at the same time opening a door so your prospect can voice another need.

Q: You're correct, we do charge more than similar companies; ten percent more, in fact. We also deliver weekly rather than monthly and have a

You're confronting the objection with absolute honesty, minimizing it and isolating the

record of absolute reliability, as these letters show. Of course there's a price tag on that kind of service. Isn't it important to you to have your deadlines met quickly and consistently?

competitive advantage you can provide, and presenting proof of your claim.

Here is another example of a way to meet objections. The scenario also illustrates how to blend customer needs with product or service features and benefits.

SCENARIO III.

In this scenario, Lisa, an educational materials sales representative, is about to make a sales pitch to the representatives of a remedial reading department of a school. They are Jane, the director, and Ralph, her assistant. The setting is the director's office.

The opening, transition, and initial pitch have taken place. There has been a discussion of the department's needs for the school year, and Lisa has shown samples of her product, a new remedial reading book series. Her goal is to sell three hundred of these kits to the school.

LISA: This is our new remedial reading kit. I know that in the lab you're talking about, your students read on about a fourth grade level. This kit is written on a second- to fourth-grade reading level and would be very appropriate for your students. It would meet the goals you've mentioned: comprehension, finding the main idea, and character development. Its content consists mostly of short stories, ideal for students like yours whose attention span is short.

Plays back and *summarizes* prospect's needs; *blends* product features and *benefits* with department's *needs*.

JANE: You know, I hate these books. They're not good literature. Why are we giving the kids such junk?

Objection.

RALPH: These kids are not going to read good literature. This junk is all they want because it relates to them. It uses the kind of language and characters they can understand.

Lisa is silent, knowing Ralph will intervene on behalf of his own interests. He does and makes a selling point.

LISA: Yes, that's right.

Supports prospect's statement.

JANE: The paper it's printed on is terrible. Not only does it yellow right away, you can see through the other side.

Valid *objection.*

LISA: That may very well be the case and the reason it's printed on this kind of paper is so we can sell it at such a low price. If it were on better paper, it would cost too much and you wouldn't be able to use it at all. Not only that, this isn't a basic reading series. It's designed to grab the interest of the slow learners, who aren't known for treating their books with any care. We put our money into grabbing the kids' attention. That's what you really want, isn't it?

Honest response. Blends objection to poor quality with *advantageous* feature.

Adds a *benefit.*

Seeks *agreement.*

RALPH: That's exactly what we want.

Agreement

LISA: So it doesn't really matter about the paper, does it?

Summarizes for *agreement.*

JANE: Well, no, but I would prefer better paper.

Objection diminished.

LISA: I agree with you. I'd prefer it, too, but this is what we have for the price, and it is the kind of reading material you need.

Makes customer right and *shares taste* in quality. *Reinforces* selling rationale.

JANE: That makes sense. If the kids like this kind of book, it will develop their reading skills and increase their interest in reading other books.

Objection overcome. Prospect mentions *benefit.*

LISA:	So these really meet your needs, don't they? If we put one into each school, it comes to about $20,000.	*Confirms* product's advantage to school reading department. Begins *trial close* by *exploring* budget capability.
RALPH:	Oh! We only have a $30,000 budget. How can we spend two-thirds of the budget on these books!	*Objection* to price.
LISA:	Well, you need these kits and you need one for every lab, so you need to buy the whole series. There's nothing else around that you can get for this kind of price.	*Overcoming objection* by restating prospect's need and *limiting their options*.
JANE:	I wish we had the money for it.	Expresses *desire*.
LISA:	If you take the kits, I can get you some additional kits from another reading level at no cost—enough to fill the needs of twenty more schools.	*Adds to advantage* of buying the kits by offering to fill *additional need at no cost*.
JANE:	That would be ideal.	The *turning point* of the sale has been reached.
LISA:	We can put one in every lab, then. Do you want me to send the kits out now? Can you get me a purchase order?	*Closes in* on their interest. *Limits choice to when,* not *Yes* or *No*.
JANE:	Now wait, I don't have the money yet.	
RALPH:	I have some money. We could split the billing between our budgets; we buy the same materials anyway.	Customer finds a way.
LISA:	Why don't I send the whole order of three hundred kits. Ralph can pay his share now, and we'll delay the rest of the billing until your money comes in, Jane.	*Begins closing* sale by negotiating agreeable payment schedule, rather than waiting for total budget and probably losing sale.

JANE:	That would be fine. But Lorna isn't here to fill in the purchase order now.

LISA:	Tell you what. You give me a purchase order and I'll sit down and fill it in. And I'll walk it through the board for you as well, so you can have the first half paid for. I'll have the entire shipment to you in three weeks.	*Closes sale* and offers *personal help* in order to expedite conclusion. Finalizes terms of *negotiation* to *close sale*.

HANDLING OBJECTIONS WHEN THE PRODUCT IS YOU

When a job, raise, or promotion is on your agenda, the techniques for handling objections are the same as when you are selling a tangible product or another kind of service. Consider how these typical objections are met in this scenario.

SCENARIO IV.

You say your budget is too tight at this time? Is that your main objection, or is there something else that bothers you?	*Explore* to find other *needs you can fill.* You may learn that your prospect isn't sure you have had enough experience; then you can produce documentary *evidence* that you have.
If I understand you correctly, you already have a good photographer on tap. Can that person also do setups, or do you have to hire a stylist in addition?	*Explore* to find a *competitive advantage* you can offer.
I know how you feel, that you don't really want to hire another photographer because it would add procedural steps and be bothersome. Actually, I have excellent sources for procuring all the equipment I'll need and will take care of it for you. So you see, your purchasing department won't have to become involved.	*Make it easy* for the prospect to buy your service.

You're correct, I do want a bigger raise than you've given your other photographers; ten percent bigger, in fact. I also know how to research each project of yours and have a record of never missing a deadline, as these letters from your clients prove. Of course, there's a price tag on that kind of service. Isn't it important to you to have your research and deadline needs met reliably and consistently?

Ask for what you are worth.

Back your request with reasons why, the *benefit* you have to offer. Offer proof.

NEGOTIATING: COMING TO TERMS

Once you have gotten the signal that your prospect is interested and agrees that he or she wants your product, service, or yourself, it's time to negotiate the sale. "Negotiating" means establishing the terms: how many, when, at what price, what title you'll have ... the specific details you'll both need to agree on to conclude the deal.

Negotiation can be a very brief phase involving short, direct, factual questions and answers. It can take longer if you need to overcome additional objections, explore further, or come up with alternative solutions. When negotiating occurs before you have gotten a commitment to buy, the naming of prices and terms limits your prospect's choices and makes it easier for him or her to reach the decision to buy or order. "Should I put you down for a dozen of these?" opens the door to *Yes,* or "A half dozen is enough right now," or "I think we can use two dozen."

When there is indecision—"I don't know. A dozen sounds good, but I just don't know."—you can get off the *Maybe* and move matters along by presenting a choice between two things: "Can you use one dozen or two?" "Should I start work here on the first or the fifteenth?" People like to have guidance; presenting clear options provides it.

Negotiating may feel to you like taking an outrageous risk. Don't be afraid of it. And don't be too modest about what you ask for. If you start high—with a large sum, an entire service package rather than a single piece, a whole shipment instead of a minimal order—you can always come down. It doesn't work well the other way around. Once you've presented a low or medium term, it's extremely difficult, in the same presentation, to ask for more.

The direct stimulus of discussing prices, delivery dates, quantities, or your title, salary, or pension plan can produce the action you're aiming at. Remember, asking for action is the ultimate goal of a presentation—whether the action is an order or another appointment.

Sometimes negotiating comes directly out of handling objections, as in the following.

SCENARIO V.

CAST.	Margo, owner of a computer software company. Doris, prospective purchaser of the company.
SETTING.	Margo's office
SYNOPSIS.	Margo's company is only two years old and has just begun to show a profit. Because of other circumstances, she wants to sell the company and has been talking for three months with a potential purchaser, Doris.
	Doris has been hemming and hawing, stuck in a *Maybe* routine. Last time they met, Margo put a time limit on the *Maybe's,* pressing for a *Yes* or a *No,* and convinced Doris to agree to investigate by December. At the current meeting, Margo has opened by asking the results of Doris's investigation.

DORIS:	I've looked into the potential of your company very thoroughly, Margo, and in view of the investment that would be required of me at this time, my answer is *No.* I'm just not in a position to make the expenditure.	*Objection* because of cost.
MARGO:	What I hear you saying is that in terms of making a large investment at this time, you are not willing to do so. Is that your main objection or is there something else that bothers you?	*Summarizes* for clarification. *Explores* for other *problems.*

DORIS:	You're correct. I'm not in a position to make a large investment right now. I also have some doubts as to how this business will take off.	*Information* about other problems.
MARGO:	Is there anything else about it that you object to?	*Assumes nothing; explores* for further information.
DORIS:	No, there isn't. You have a splendid organization and a great facility. It's probably just what I want, but right now I don't want to make the investment.	Evidence of *interest* and *desire;* primary objection still stands, with added *information,* "right now."
MARGO:	When do you feel that you would be willing to make it?	*Plays back* "right now" and *limits answer* to "when," not "if."
DORIS:	That would be when I think it's closer to taking off.	Inconclusive; *"Maybe."*
MARGO:	Let's see what we have here. It's an ideal situation. Our organization and facility are excellent, and it's probably just the kind of business you want. You don't have the money to invest in it right now, but you might in the future. And you're not quite sure how it will operate. Let me see if I can come up with an alternate plan, so you can see if it is for you. I'd be willing to have you rent the facility, using my personnel, on a trial basis. If it works out well for you, then we can talk about a financial investment further down the line. If it doesn't work out, you will have had a trial balloon and I will have gained	*Summarizes* positive points. The peg to deal from. *Offers* to help Doris make a decision by *negotiation* of a compromise solution. *Offers deal* without cost or risk; sets up *win–win situation.*

	something, too. How does that concept feel to you?	*Asks* for trial order.
DORIS:	I hadn't considered that. It sounds very good. What kind of rental are we talking about?	Prospect is now actively involved in buying decision.

What Margo did was explore Doris's objections to make them crystal clear, and then offer an alternative plan that both women could live with. She changed *Maybe* and *No* into a probable *Yes*, which will be a complete win–win situation. Even if the *Maybe* remains *No*, Margo will be in an improved situation. Given a decision that completes the cycle, she will be free to move on to the next prospective buyer. And this discussion has now led to a discussion of terms.

SCENARIO VI.

In the scenario that follows, Kate, a financial analyst, and Steven, a bank officer, have agreed that Kate will assist Steven on a special project. She has basically made the sale but her fee has not yet been discussed—and the sale will not be final until it is.

KATE:	Steven, there is something we haven't gotten around to: my compensation. I am more than happy to assist you on this project, but I think we should agree on terms now, before we get too deeply into the work.	Speaks about money *directly and openly,* without apology or nervousness.
STEVEN:	Of course.	
KATE:	Since I am the expert in this area and we agree I'm the person to help, what do you think would be an appropriate fee?	Establishes her *ability to fill his need* and implies that she is worth a significant fee. Gives him the opportunity to *inform* her of what range he has in mind.
STEVEN:	Well, I don't have a huge budget, but I do need your help. I think $300 a day on a per diem basis is about right.	Gives *information* about price range.

KATE:	Steven, my regular fee is $600 a day. I estimate this project will take approximately six days of my time, so the total would be $3,600.	Begins *negotiating* process, starting higher than what she will accept, to leave room for discussion and win–win agreement.
STEVEN:	I'm sorry. We have no intention of paying that much. It's out of the question; we never pay $600 fees. The highest we've ever paid is $500 a day.	*Objection.* Provides solid *information* Kate can work with.
KATE:	My regular fee is $600. However, since $500 is the most you have paid to date and since I know you'll be pleased with my work, I'd be willing to compromise this once at $550, on condition that on my next project for you my fee is the regular $600.	*Negotiates* downward gradually, so she won't conclude deal below her minimum of $500, and setting up bigger fee for future projects.
STEVEN:	I'm afraid $500 is our absolute tops, Kate, and I don't know that we could ever go up to $600.	He has gone from $300 to $500.
KATE:	Alright. Let's do this one at your top figure of $500, and then we can negotiate in good faith when the next project comes around.	She has gotten the $500 she wanted by coming down from $600.
STEVEN:	That sounds very fair. I'll have a letter of agreement drawn up and it will be on your desk by Tuesday.	They both have what they want. It is a *win–win* situation.

CLOSING THE SALE

At the point when you have aroused definite interest, close the deal. Briefly, confirm where you and your prospect stand by summarizing the points you have agreed on and the important benefits you will provide. Be direct about asking for the order or action you came for, and ask for it with the positive attitude that the sale is yours.

What you're looking for is definite action; you want a *Yes* or a *No*. Asking for that action is where most women fall apart. They're afraid to take the risk of hearing *No*. That doesn't make much sense when you stop and realize that unless you ask for action, all the work you've done so far will be useless. A *No* isn't going to kill you; it will complete the cycle for you and at the same time give you the opportunity to ask, "Why '*No*'?" and then clarify any possible misinterpretation.

The worst word you can hear is *Maybe*. If that's what you get when you ask for action, just keep on going until you get a definite *Yes* or *No*.

Closing is hard because you're asking for a commitment. The way to make it easier is to come from a positive attitude that, of course, your prospect will agree with your point of view. Ask for the commitment in a positive way: "When shall I start? If you sign these papers now, I can begin next Monday." "I'll have my office prepare the plans and I can get them to you by Wednesday. I'll need your signature to get that into motion." "From everything we've spoken about, this sounds like it's my job. You like the approach, you're confident I can help you, all that remains is signing the papers and setting the date for when you'd like me on board."

Here's an illustration of how one sale was closed.

SCENARIO VII. CLOSING THE SALE.

CAST.	Andrea, a fund-raiser for Ivy University. She is wearing a conservative print dress that is womanly but not sexy, low-key but fashionable. It is a presence her prospect can feel comfortable with. Ruth, prospective donor, widow of Ivy alumnus.
SETTING.	Ruth's living room.
SYNOPSIS.	Andrea's goal is a $5,000 donation. She has asked Ruth for $5,000 to $7,000 to equip an Ivy gymnasium. Ruth has agreed that equipment is needed but was thinking of donating $3,000. She is not sure about making a donation at this point and is at the *Maybe* stage.
ANDREA:	I want to tell you how very pleased I am with your *Summarizes* position.

enormous enthusiasm for Ivy
University. From everything
you've said, you see as clearly
as we do the need for
additional equipment for the
gymnasium. I think it would   *Benefit* that appeals
be very appropriate to   to the prospect's *ego.*
purchase that equipment
in your husband's name and
to place a plaque on the
storage area dedicating it to   Makes it *real* by
him. Let's think about   visualizing appearance
what the plaque should   of plaque.
say.

RUTH: I like the idea of having a   *Agreement.*
plaque in my husband's name.
I think it should be quite   Plaque has *reality.*
small, with very contemporary
lettering.

ANDREA: By small, would you say ten   Bolstering *reality*
inches, or twelve or sixteen?   and making it difficult
How do you see it?   for prospect to back off.

RUTH: I'd like something very small,
very discreet. I was thinking
of a ten-inch plaque.

ANDREA: Let's see what it will say, so   *Solidifying* reality.
we'll know if the ten inches
will take care of it. We'll
write it out. I can see the
plaque very fittingly in the   Appeal to emotions.
East Gymnasium, where your
husband used to watch
basketball.

RUTH: You are so right.

ANDREA: In order to equip that gym   Starts *negotiation* with
properly, it would take $7,000   figure higher than goal.
worth of equipment.

RUTH: As I told you, Andrea, $3,000   Is out of *Maybe* and into
is what I'm prepared to give.   *Yes.* Only terms remain
                                    for concluding.

ANDREA: That's so. Why don't we pick a figure in between the two. If you put in $5,000, I know of some extra funds that can fill out the rest. And the equipment will still be a gift in your husband's memory. Would you like to give us a check or shall we purchase the equipment and have you billed directly?

Starts to complete *negotiation*. Makes it easy for Ruth to *agree* on $5,000, adds *emotional appeal* to seal the idea.
Limits choice to two.

RUTH: Have them bill me direct, please.

The sale is *closed*.

ANDREA: Fine. What I need is your authorization. I'll write up an agreement that you are to fund new equipment for the East Gym in an amount not to exceed $5,000. That sum includes the plaque, of course. Let's write out the wording for the plaque, to be sure the spelling is correct; then you can sign the agreement and we will proceed according to your wishes.

Completes *closing sale* in writing.

GET IT IN WRITING

Once you have closed a sale, be sure you have the agreement in writing, either a contract or a letter of agreement that incorporates all the terms you have settled on: how, when, where, what the project is, the financial terms, everything you've closed on. Spell out each term clearly, so there will be no unpleasant surprises later on and so that you will have something to refer to should a question or a problem ever arise.

EXTENDING THE SALE

You can extend your sales even when you're dealing with what may seem to be a single item. If you're an automobile salesperson, for example, you can pitch accessories for the car, once you have evoked strong interest, and are at the closing stage. "You'll want an FM radio, of course, and how about a tape deck to break up those long trips you take? You really ought to have whitewalls, too; they add such a distinctive look." If you're a boutique salesperson, you'll want to extend your clothing sales by suggesting accessories: "This scarf really completes the look you're after—it's perfect with this dress. Try it on, tied and twisted this way!"

To extend the sale when you're in a service business and already have sufficient proof of performance so you're beyond selling one-shots to build up validation, you can ask for a retainer and offer a package of ongoing work, instead of the single project you've discussed. But you have to ask. It's up to you to take the initiative if you're going to extend a sale—even though you may be accustomed to the passive position of responding to other people's suggestions instead of initiating the action. That is one of the major differences between men and women: Men are active, while women traditionally back down. It's also one of the major differences between succeeding and not succeeding in the selling game.

You can take the lead and extend your sale when you're selling yourself, also, although there's a bigger risk involved. Unless you have very strong credentials behind you, you may lose everything you've just won if you ask for the moon. In extending the sale of a service or yourself, be realistic about whether you really are worth more than the competition. And be sure that strong interest in you has been established. Here are two situations to illustrate the point:

Sheila was looking for her very first job. She had excellent credentials—a master's degree and all sorts of recommendations from influential contacts—and was obviously extremely bright. She was inexperienced in the business world, but confident of her ability. A contact had spoken to the vice president of a small computer firm about Sheila, and an interview was arranged. The vice president showed a strong interest in hiring her, then asked what she thought her salary should be. Sheila went for broke, asking $32,000—double the amount she thought someone just out of college could command.

When he agreed, greed got a hold of her. She tried to extend the sale by asking for a three-week paid vacation her first year there and a guaranteed bonus at Christmas time. At that point, the vice president backed off from hiring Sheila. She would have done better not trying to extend her sale to this extent on her first job, but waiting until she had experience to negotiate effectively.

Beth, on the other hand, has been a free-lance marketing consultant for 15 years and has gained recognition for proven excellence in her field. When a large manufacturer asked her to provide a new product survey in test market areas, she told him:

> I'm pleased that you've come to me. I do test surveys all the time and I know it's one of the minor segments of a problem such as yours. You need to know how to position and market your product, as well. I wouldn't feel right only selling you a test survey and then leaving you out there without the follow-through, in a position of possible failure because you lack complete data.
>
> I strongly urge that you hire me on retainer to administer the entire package you need, so your new product will succeed.

At this point the manufacturer could have turned on his heel, interested in contracting for test survey or nothing. Or he could have bought Beth's extended idea of a complete marketing package because of her successful track record and outstanding professional expertise. Beth was gambling, and she won.

One of the most obvious areas for extending sales is the field of cosmetics sales. Here the goal for the salesperson is to sell an entire line and to "bond" customers to her for ongoing repeat sales. This scenario provides an excellent illustration of extending a sale.

SCENE VIII. EXTENDING A SALE.

CAST.	Sara, a cosmetics salesperson. Ms. Brown, customer.	
SETTING.	A department store cosmetics counter.	
SYNOPSIS.	Customer walks slowly to counter, browsing.	
SARA:	Hello, my name is Sara. I see you're interested in our new fall line. Would you like to try on that lipstick? It's from our new "Tawny"	Introduces self to establish friendly contact. *Explores* customer's interest and urges action (Opening with "May

	line for fall and it would be very flattering to your skin tone.	I help you?" would have gotten a *Yes* or *No* and left no room for probing the the customer's interest.)
MS. BROWN:	Oh, I'm just browsing.	
SARA:	Fine. It's one of those cool, cloudy fall days when you feel like being indoors.	Relaxes customer with *small talk* on unrelated subject.
MS. BROWN:	Is this the new shade you advertised?	Customer no longer intimidated by the presence of fashion authority.
SARA:	Yes, it is. This lipstick is great—our newest moisturizing formula, and the color actually stays on for eight hours. Let me try this cinnamon-y orange on you. Everyone loves the texture.	Presents *selling feature.* Works to arouse desire.
MS. BROWN:	Yes, it's quite creamy.	*Agreement.*
SARA:	And another great thing about it is that it lasts and looks this fresh all day. You'll get good wear out of it. You can also try one of our tinted lip glosses to apply over it, which gives you a beautiful dewy look for evening.	*Supports* first *selling feature* and adds another. *Extending* the sale.
MS. BROWN:	I don't like lip gloss. It's too gooey.	*Objection.*
SARA:	You can use the lipstick by itself, as you like. It does have a nice shine to it because of the moisturizers in it. How do you like it?	Customer is always *right.* Reinforces basic *selling point. Probing* for problems and needs.
MS. BROWN:	It looks quite nice.	*Interest, desire, agreement.*

SARA: We also have a blush to coordinate with that shade. It's a natural-looking rust that would really complement the lipstick and highlight your own coloring, too. Let me put it on for you.

Appeal to ego. If she tries *it, she's more apt to buy it.*

MS. BROWN: It looks pretty good.

Interest, desire, agreement.

SARA: Let me show you the matching nail polish. It makes for such a finished look.

Extending the sale. Trying to get customer to try entire line.

MS. BROWN: I never wear nail polish.

Objection.

SARA: You never wear nail polish? But you have such lovely hands.

Tries to overcome objection by appeal to ego.

MS. BROWN: I hate nail polish and my husband hates it, too.

Objection.

SARA: I see. Perhaps there is something else you can use today. We have a half-price special on our eye shadows. You can get the fabulous six-shade "Tawny Pack," which is usually $15, for only $7.50.

Extending sale.

Appeal to price-saving.

MS. BROWN: I don't think I need shadow. I have so many at home.

Objection.

SARA: Our "Year 3000 Moisturizer" is on sale today. It's also half price.

MS. BROWN: I'm still using one I have at home.

SARA: You have one you're using? Fine. When you finish it, do come back and see me because I think you'd be very excited about ours. It's got a great anti-aging

Meets objection with *promise of benefit.*

	formula—little lines and dry skin patches seem to disappear from your skin for hours.	
MS. BROWN:	Thanks, I'll just take the lipstick and blusher today.	Makes *decision.* *Sale closed.*
SARA:	Thank you. Please do come back and see me because we get new shades and products all the time. And if you ever have a problem, I'll be happy to help you. Here's a card with my name and phone number. I'll also put you on my follow-up list and call you in a month to see how you're doing and if you need a new moisturizer.	Leaves customer with feeling of friendship and *support* plus reason to come back. *Makes it easy* for customer to repeat purchase.

Once you've closed the sale and perhaps extended it, assure your client or customer of your friendship and sincerity, support the wisdom of the decision he or she has made—and leave. You both have other things to do with the selling cycle complete.

> **Reality:** *The difference between major success and just getting by is a matter of two or three extra sales pitches a week.*

THE FOLLOW-UP: HOW TO KEEP ON GETTING WHAT YOU WANT

Being a success at selling is like being a successful friend: You need to keep right on being attentive after the sale has been closed. You cement the relationship by showing courtesy and friendship. You encourage the other person's confidence in you and what you can do. You're understanding, you're helpful, you never let him or her forget you. In other words, you keep on selling after the sale has been made, to keep the rapport you've established alive and healthy.

There's a chain of good reasons for continuing to be attentive so people will keep asking for what you've got. First, by keeping the lines of communication open, you keep gaining information about how to extend the sale. Second, by keeping the door open, you build your network of contacts. Some people call this "using the user." It is! A satisfied customer, client, or employer is the best lead you can have to other new customers, clients, or employers.

And since relocation because of a job change has become customary for so many people, maintaining a connection with that customer need not mean a loss of business: It can add to your income possibilities. As *they* move around and work with other companies, they can expand your income-making possibilities if you keep in touch with them. It requires more follow-through—but it's *worth your effort.*

> **Reality:** *It takes more time and effort to develop a new client than to hang onto an old one.*

HOW IT FEELS
TO HAVE WHAT
YOU WANT

There are rewards for success, there are prices for success, and there are choices we must make as we strive for success. As women, we're still learning what the rewards, prices, and choices are all about. Among the joys of success is the great feeling of accomplishment and, with it, the ability and privilege of helping others to succeed.

We have a generation of pathfinders now who've broken lots of what was thought to be impenetrable ground and who have become role models or mentors for other women. The rewards and accomplishments women made in the Industrial Age are increasing, but also shifting and changing, as we move through the Information Age and into the twenty-first century.

Women are still new to the professional-success game, even as gender roles are changing. There's a trade-off for everything and a price to be paid for success. Juggling the roles of wife, mother, and career woman often means that you have to give up long-standing customs and relationships. The changes in lifestyle may unbalance a marriage, alter your status in the community, and affect the way other people react to your multifaceted "superwoman" personality. There are inevitable strains put on love relationships and marriages in a two-career alliance. This is a fact of life—even decades into women's march to work, men are still threatened by women who strive and compete.

If a successful career is your goal, not just a day job to help pay the bills, understand that there will be some price to pay in your personal life, more often than not. Hopefully, you'll be one of the lucky women like, for instance, Hillary Clinton, who is married to a man more successful than she, but a man who does not ask her to be less so he can look like more.

And remember that, if you are successful, there are all sorts of rewards you can count.

> **Reality:** *Every situation breeds a set of problems. It's a matter of which set of problems you would rather have.*

THE PRICE OF SUCCESS

The price of success varies with the individual, but almost no woman's life is left unchanged by her striving for a career. Sometimes the price feels overwhelming, as Laura, a 52-year-old publisher, reports:

> I paid for my success—it cost me one marriage and the second is on the edge of breaking up. I paid for it by working without the support of people close to me. My parents, who are in their 70s, are supportive now, but they weren't for a long time. They didn't understand what I was working so hard for. My mother would say, "Why work? Take care of yourself and get married."
>
> I did get married, at 22. I followed the program totally and had my children right away. I was miserable. So when I was 31 I was divorced, with two young children. I knew what I really wanted to do when I was 18 and it was what I had to do now. But there was no one to encourage me 30 years ago.
>
> Consciousness is more evolved now and women are growing up more aware of options; they don't have to buy into the cultural stereotypes of women or be damned, as I did and I was, when I was 22. Women have choices and it's an accepted fact that they do.
>
> I don't regret having my children, and I don't regret choosing to make a professional life for myself, but I do regret that I never met a man who could accept me—and my ambition—in one package.

Laura still feels hurt by her failed and failing marriages, and it's hard on her. She says she's "in a whole role-reversal" with her husband, Richard, in which she's virtually "the mythological man and he is the fabled dependent woman." She continues her story:

> Richard will not accept a not-so-new cultural concept already—women wanting to work at careers is not news any more. But for him, it's *personal*. For me there is the very real joy of professional satisfaction after years of struggle, and I won't give it up, not even to satisfy Richard's ego.
>
> I grew up with the belief in *sharing* who you are and what you make of yourself with someone you care about, and vice versa. I never expected that the person I want to share my success with would be scared by it.

Her success is eroding Laura's second marriage, but not to pay that price of loss is, she says, "far more catastrophic. Because to play out somebody else's script is to do your own development a disservice."

Family life is rarely unaffected by a woman's efforts to achieve career success. Sometimes roles must be renegotiated; other times they shift in ways that have not been anticipated. Patti says:

> I've stopped making big dinners every night and hired someone to come in and clean six hours a week. Oddly enough, my kids give me total support, but my husband still yearns for the *I Love Lucy* model of wifeliness he watches in the reruns. I think he's typical of many men who still give lip service to women's interests. Intellectually, they think what we're doing is terrific, but down deep, they want us back on the "Mommy track"—total caretaking.
>
> I have an ongoing fight with Jack that shows what I mean. He traveled five months in the first year of our marriage and never once was concerned about how I was going to manage my business and the house and all the problems that came up while he was away. Now, if I'm away for one evening, he's furious. He accepts what I do so grudgingly, and resents it.
>
> It's taken me a lot of looking in the mirror and saying, "Keep going. I'm not guilty," because if don't, I'll give in to him and sell my business. I can't let that happen.

Sometimes the price is in coping with other people's reactions to your success. It's interesting that most often it is men who cannot accept a woman's professional development, but other women may not be delighted, either. Janet, the owner of an interior design business, told me:

> I cannot tell you the number of men who have made jealous remarks: "Oh, good for you—now you're going to be rich, right?" They don't do it to put me down necessarily; they're just uncomfortable when they hear of my success.
>
> On the other hand, most women I know—not only my women friends but the women who work with me—are generally pleased and happy for me. Of course there are competitive women who are careerists for themselves only, and can be brutal obstacle builders along your path.
>
> I just feel sorry for men or women who live and think these short-sighted ways.

THE WAGES OF LEARNING TO SELL

Salespeople have been the butt of many jokes over the years —so many, in fact, that their image has become tarnished in some circles. For many women, learning that selling is what business is all about is a rude jolt. Perhaps this is because while women sell themselves every day of their personal lives, their efforts in the business world are contrary to some of their cultural conditioning.

For many women, learning to sell involves confronting subconscious motivations, redirecting talents and skills that they have been taught were best left lying partially submerged. The following excerpts describe how many women have successfully come to terms with the necessity of selling themselves, their products, or their services and how they have put their skills and talents to work to get exactly what they want from life in a direct, up-front manner.

CHANGING ATTITUDES

Georgette, who is now earning about $150,000 a year in network marketing, told me:

I went into the field of network sales thinking it was very de-
meaning. I had no respect for it—the lowest of the low, just
something I was doing to get out of teaching. In the beginning, I
loved the selling, the meetings, the way the business worked, although I couldn't understand why. I thought it was such a trivial,
meaningless occupation, so how could I like it? Finally I decided that this ridiculous prejudice had to go.

Network sales was a perfectly valuable way to make a living—
exciting and stimulating. Maybe it was the way I was brought
up, feeling that being in a profession like teaching or law is the
only worthwhile thing, that made me come to sales feeling it
was beneath me. Now I'm successful at it. I've learned to push
the issues, to handle objections, to motivate others in my network, to recruit.

I've learned that this is business and if I want to succeed, I've got
to play it the way it works.

I had a lot of sleepless nights when I started. I felt that I was giving up too much: Other women were out dating while I was out
organizing network parties and traveling, sometimes a thousand
miles from home, to follow up on what I felt would be the killer
recruit—someone I'd want working with and for me.

I really feel I have a purpose, and that's made the struggle pay off.

Regina, who sells costume jewelry to department stores and
boutiques for a very widely-distributed designer, told her story:

When I was a child, I'd play precious little girl just to win my
mother's favor or get my father's attention. I couldn't have the
world know me for what I was, faults and all. I had to become
what the world wanted. It took a lot of growing up to learn that
I could just be myself, without having to be a "pleaser."

I think that being in sales made me grow up. You get to deal
with a lot of reality when you're selling. You get to know people as they really are behind their masks, and they get to see
you as you really are, too. You have to be honest about yourself
as well as about what you're selling, and the realization that
honesty is okay is one of the best things that has happened in
my life.

Tina, who sells for a large Midwestern printing company, said:

I talk to myself a lot. I call it making a positive self-presentation. From talking to a number of other women, I imagine that I'm not alone in doing this. Because no matter how qualified we are, no matter how many degrees we have, no matter how much experience we have, there's a little voice in there that picks on our weak points and insecurities. Actor Carrie Fisher once said in an interview that for a long time, she'd jump right in a conversation and put herself down before "other people had a chance" to get there first.

For me, it's never feeling that I'm quite good enough; maybe I didn't say the right things; I could have handled that a little differently or done this a bit better. I'm changing and starting to think, "Well, that's the way it was. Just move on and make it better next time." Turning all those negatives around really has helped my frame of mind. I've also learned that when you're doing my kind of sales, you can't please everyone—and you can't take it personally. So you talk to yourself in a very positive way, focusing on your strengths. You build on these instead of dwelling on your shortcomings.

Getting it straightened out has given me so much confidence. Instead of thinking, "They don't want me," I think, "Look what I have to offer." For me, self-awareness and taking responsibility for myself are important. Grasp the fact that you're the one in total control of your life and once you understand that, you can have what you want.

Susan, who is a vice president at a company that does merchandising related to sports, said:

I had to work my way through the ego part of competing with other salespeople in the company. I had to decide that there would be times when I would be on top, and there would be times when the other salespeople would knock me off my perch. It was nice for them when they did well and it was nice for me when I did well.

What I finally worked through is managing my competitive edge—to ease up on the drive that makes me always want to be first.

Sharon, a former human resources executive who was recruited into network marketing and who has done very well, said:

I grew up as a "princess." That's someone who spends her time trying to get her way—and getting the material things she thinks she's entitled to—in one way or another. The "ways" are wheedling, manipulating, or whatever she thinks it takes.

This demanding manner is something I've always been aware of and don't like in myself. But it's always been there. It's there when I sell, because sales is manipulation—you're persuading people to do what you want, to buy what you're selling, maybe even reluctantly. Now that I talk about it, maybe being a princess isn't as bad as I fear it was!

Once you get the ball rolling, the ability to sell can be one of your strongest personal assets. Knowing what you are worth in the marketplace and making use of your value is an invigorating experience, as Paula tells it:

Once I started selling, my confidence in myself grew. If I still felt about myself the way I used to, I wouldn't have what I have now because I didn't *give* anything. Let me clarify that.

I more or less had an inferiority complex, and it would get in my way because I was so involved in feeling inadequate, I couldn't give anything to anybody. Once I got over this, things started rolling.

Selling got me out of my shyness. I got a job representing a pharmaceuticals manufacturer, where I was forced to deal with the public in situations that were different from any I'd been in. I found out when you're dealing with so many total strangers every day, you just can't be timid.

I made friends in business, and everybody would try to help me, giving me little hints on how to talk to people, how to get what you want. It's been a great learning experience for me. I still have a way to go, because there's a lot more I want to get out and do. Most of all, I feel good about myself.

THE REWARDS OF SUCCESS

The rewards of finding out what it is you want to do in life and then setting out purposefully to accomplish your goal are wonderfully self-satisfying, as Betty, a late-blooming entrepreneur, discovered:

There's a vision to keep when you are a kid in terms of what's possible for you out there. I'm 47 and I bounce out of bed every morning filled with energy. Every day feels like I've got the Hubbel Telescope and I can look out there into the universe and decide where I want to land—and where to colonize.

Once you realize that most anything is possible, there are no restrictions on you except those you put on yourself. Every day is an adventure, which is not to say that every day is fun. There are plenty of nights when I come home and cry, eat half a box of Oreos, and fight with my husband or drop into bed at seven because I'm so exhausted. Being in business may not be easy, but it's never dull.

Today was incredible. I sold a project I've been working on for years, and it's going to be the biggest success of my life. I came home absolutely exhausted with joy. I think I could have made it happen sooner if I'd believed in myself more, and sooner.

Four years ago I knew I was good enough—and I had paid my dues. I had been working steadily, but I was like a kid with my nose pressed against the glass, watching others with less talent, less smarts, get the kudos.

The project I just recently sold came when I realized that a lot of old emotional and professional baggage that was holding me back had to be thrown out. To succeed, I had to hard-sell my big idea and believe I was entitled to success. I was as talented as anybody around my company. So to win, I had to sit down and figure out my strategy to get what I wanted.

My answer was *confidence and attitude*. I knew I had to get something different into my tone that people would hear. That's what selling is about: to believe in what you're selling without apology. To believe passionately that what you're selling is worth something, and that you are worthy of selling it. From there, you go to work on the specifics of the selling situation you're in.

An attitude change did it for me—what a revelation!

MEASURING WHAT SUCCESS WILL COST YOU

Measuring the price of your success before you have achieved it is very much like planning goals. What you think you may be giving up may not have to be sacrificed at all, and something you imagined would not change may well turn topsy-turvy overnight. But if you know yourself well, you'll be able to outline what you think success will cost and what its rewards will be.

Think carefully about what success will mean to you and make a balance sheet. Write down what you think its costs and rewards will be to you. Then, as you come closer to achieving your goal, look at your list again and reevaluate your feelings about success. Are the costs acceptable? Are the rewards sufficient? Would you willingly do what you've done all over again?

It helps to force yourself to define what's happening in your life and how you really feel about it. The greatest help may be when the bottom line of your balance sheet reads, "Stop bitching and start winning!"

FINALLY ...

I want to leave you with a brief tale of spectacular success in how *selling an idea,* which became the sale of the century, changed the world in less than a decade. It's about Bill Gates, founder of Microsoft and the world's richest private citizen with a fortune estimated at $20 billion. Gates is considered a rare breed—a genius at invention and development of an idea, having a vision that he can sell to others, and being a brilliant businessman. He's also got a reputation for being *pushy* about his business.

Newsjournalist Tom Brokaw asked Gates in an interview about his "triple threat" talents and his aggressive selling of Microsoft and its products. Gates said that he didn't think that his style was aggressive—simply enthusiastic. *"I love what I do,"* he said, explaining that his enthusiasm and his belief in his company and what it could do may come off as overbearing. He added that he hated negotiating, which for him was the worst part of making the sale or the deal.

So, selling isn't easy. But if, like Bill Gates, you practice it; are focused, flexible, and inventive; do what you don't like because it's important and necessary; continue to set your goals; are motivated; and *love what you do*—you'll make the sale and have *your version* of success.

I hope the selling game techniques I've outlined in this book will help you move into the golden age of marketing, and bring to you all the personal and professional satisfaction imaginable.

Reality: *The best feeling in the world is winning at the woman's selling game, and nobody deserves to win more than* **you***!*

About the Author

Carole Hyatt is an internationally renowned market and social behavior researcher, lecturer, and author of the bestselling business classic, *When Smart People Fail*. She assisted Fortune 500 companies, the media, and government agencies in creating and selling hundreds of new products, programs, and services. Hyatt lives in New York City.

Carole Hyatt creates projects that integrate her varied background experiences in business, education, and theater. Her activities include motivational speaking and interactive workshops on the international circuit. She travels regularly to five continents, speaking to audiences ranging from Jamaican women small business owners to Japanese multinational business professionals.

Her books, also including *Lifetime Employability, Shifting Gears,* and *Woman & Work,* are based on case studies of prominent and typical North Americans and have been reviewed as "seminal works." As a career specialist, her speeches, lectures, and books have one overriding design: helping people get in touch with their natural gifts and skills in order to develop strategies for a fulfilling life.